ICONOGRAPHIC COLLECTIONS

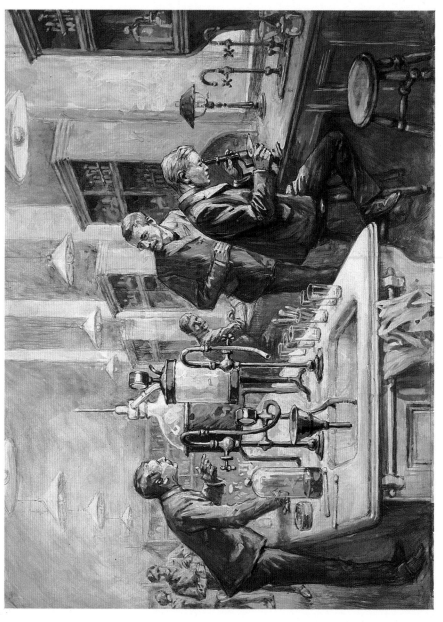

Fig. 1 a laboratory in the Liverpool School of Tropical Medicine soon after its opening in April 1899. The foreground figures are (left to right) Sir Ronald Ross, C.S. Sherrington, and Rubert W. Boyce (using microscope). See further p. 53. Gouache in grisaille on paper 29.9 × 40.7 cm. by W.T. Maud, 1899.

The Iconographic Collections

of the

Wellcome Institute for the History of Medicine

William Schupbach

1989

CONTENTS

INTRODUCTION

The unique array of paintings, drawings, photographs and prints in the Wellcome Institute Library proclaims the fact that from its earliest days the Wellcome Institute for the History of Medicine, as a centre of knowledge of medicine in its several historical roles, has embraced the *iconography* as well as the *bibliography* of the subjects in which it takes an interest. Sir Henry Solomon Wellcome's will of 29 February 1932, which is essentially the Library's charter, directs and declares that his endowment be used both for the maintenance of his existing research establishments, which included collections of pictures, and "for the purchase and acquisition of books, manuscripts, documents, pictures and other works of art" in order to enlarge and improve their holdings. The "pictures and other works of art" which are our concern in this booklet, both those already in Wellcome's possession and those acquired subsequently by his Trustees, have been collected to create a pictorial record, or iconography, of the history of medicine and related subjects. The purpose of this booklet is to offer an explanation of what this unusual (though not unique) project might mean: firstly, through a consideration of the subject-approach to pictures implicit in Wellcome's words; secondly, by showing that that approach has inspired the creation of numerous other iconographic collections in the libraries of Europe and America, each reflecting the interests of its founder and officers; thirdly, to focus on this particular collection, by answering questions as to whence, where, what and how; and lastly, by providing a basic guide to literature on medico-historical iconography as a starting-point to those minded to pursue their own studies in this field.

There are two special points of which the reader should be warned at the outset, one about language, the other about substance.

The first concerns the terms used to describe items in the Wellcome Institute's Iconographic Collections. The Greeks had a single word— εἰκών (*icon*)—which could describe any form of image, whether painting or engraving, sculpture or embroidery, mirror-image or hallucination. English has no equally comprehensive term. Our terms are specialized: "picture" and "depiction" are taken to imply paintings; "graphic art" is supposed to include only drawings and prints; "figurative" is interpreted as referring only to human figures; "illustrations" exclude items not related to texts; "images" are abstractions divorced from their medium and cannot constitute a collection; and "icons" are now associated either with religious paintings from eastern Europe or with diagrammatic constructions on computer display screens. In the absence of one comprehensive term this booklet follows English colloquial usage and uses "picture" without implying any particular medium.

Secondly, the reader will find in this booklet references to subjects and specific items which are known by the present writer to exist in the Wellcome Institute Library's collections. However, since the writer is personally familiar with only a portion of the holdings, these examples are selected without the advantage of a synoptic view of what is available. As in many large collections, much of the material is still inadequately documented, unprepared for handling or otherwise inaccessible. That enough is known of the Iconographic Collections to allow the production of this booklet is to the credit of previous curators, but since much remains to be learnt about the collections even by those in charge of them, the reader should not mistake the present superficial and provisional account for the balanced and fully informed survey which a future generation will be able to enjoy.

ICONOGRAPHY

Iconography may not be a household word but it is the *mot juste* for several related activities which have a long history.[1]* For the present purpose, it may be said by way of definition that the iconography of a given subject is its record in pictures. One obtains such a record by identifying different pictures of the same subject, distinguishing them from similar pictures of different subjects, and collecting, comparing and interpreting pictures of each subject in turn, with reference both to each other and to other historical documents. This work is intended to ensure that, when historians need to account for pictorial documents in their field, the right pictures will be known and will be brought into play together with textual and any other evidence.

To restore pictures of a subject to their place in the history of that subject as a whole, iconography reconstructs the links between the picture and the written word. The symbiosis between literary and pictorial documents which it requires is enjoyed by most great historical libraries as a matter of course, for these two kinds of record embrace each other: words are as common in pictures as pictures are in books, and there are ways of interpretation which apply equally to all humanly-produced documents, questions which historians ask about the authorship, genre, mode, formation and function of any work, literary or graphic, to be used as evidence in building up a case. William Harvey's lecture-notes, the plays of Shakespeare, the paintings of Rembrandt and the meanest anatomical diagram all, to a degree, respond to the same tactics of informed interrogation.

The first phase of iconography, *identification of the subject,* was first practised, if we are to believe the ancient Greek author Aelian, when a painter wrote "That is an ox", "That is a horse", "That is a tree" on his primitive attempts at graphic representation.[2] Since that mythical occasion, the graphic arts, literature and the relations between them have all become more sophisticated, but the work of scholars such as Aby Warburg (1866-1929)—to name one of many—has enabled the iconographer to interpret with some precision the far more elaborate subjects represented in the graphic arts from antiquity to the twentieth century, such as themes from Indian astronomy painted on the walls of an Italian palace, or the attributes of lunatics in an engraving by William Hogarth.[3] Yet even at this preliminary stage many famous works still remain undeciphered, notoriously the paintings of Hieronymus Bosch (*c.* 1450-1516), a name which is pertinent in this context because the

*For references see pp. 50-52.

3

Wellcome Institute Library has one of the three early copies of his controversial so-called "Garden of earthly delights" (fig. 2).

The second of the phases distinguished above (though it is actually simultaneous with the first) is *the collection of pictures of the same subject*. The works of iconographic scholarship which result from this activity may be collections of new pictures created for the purpose, for example the pictures of patients with nervous disorders collected in the *Nouvelle Iconographie de la Salpêtrière* by Jean-Martin Charcot and his colleagues (Paris 1888-1918). More commonly they are collections of pictures already in existence, and just as military historians are familiar with Wellesley and Steegmann's *The iconography of the first Duke of Wellington* (London 1935), and historians of religion with the series *Iconography of religions* published by the Institute of Religious Iconography, State University of Groningen, so, in the medical field, to take four examples represented in the Wellcome Institute Library, there is or could be an iconography of a practice such as bloodletting (including the picture reproduced on the front cover of this booklet), of an institution such as Bethlem Royal Hospital, of a disease such as goitre, and of a person such as the Flemish anatomist Andreas Vesalius (1514-1564). Indeed, a book entitled *The iconography of Andreas Vesalius* by M.H. Spielmann (London 1925) was one of the first major historical publications issued by Sir Henry Wellcome, the founder of the Library.

Embodying as it does the iconography of medical history and germane subjects, an iconographic collection like the Wellcome Institute's is distinguished from various kinds of art-collection by the fact that it has been created and organized primarily for the study of the subjects of its pictures, not for aesthetic pleasure nor to illustrate the history of graphic or pictorial styles as such. In addition to the major ostensible themes of a work, the subject of a picture can include overtones, allusions, suppressions, distortions, implications and assumptions, and may also be shaped by stylistic traditions, artistic flair and, often, the wiles of the market-place. Some of the legends printed or written on works of art are also inseparable from the subject.

To arrive at a full understanding of the subject, the student of pictures, whatever his or her purpose, must give due weight to connoisseurship, the history of the fine arts, linguistic knowledge and other skills appropriate to the interpretation of pictures. No collection of pictures can be justified through iconography alone. The discovery of the authorship, date or original setting of a picture must be allowed to influence one's interpretation of its subject. The content of an anatomical illustration may vary according to whether it was addressed to a popular or to a learned audience, and therefore needs more than

Fig. 2 a reduced copy by an unknown painter, perhaps a Fleming active in the mid-sixteenth century, of the central panel of a triptych by Hieronymus Bosch (c. 1450-1516), which is now in the Museo del Prado, Madrid. Among the profusion of themes which may be found in the picture, it was probably the ideas of primitivism, ritual, ethnicity, nudity, and the ever-problematic relations between man, beast and plant, which attracted Wellcome to the picture. See further p. 53.

The composition has been referred to by many different names ("El tráfago del mundo", "Die Weltlust", "De tuin der lusten", "The garden of earthly delights" etc.), their variety reflecting both the plethora of scenes within the picture and uncertainty of their combined significance. These names, however, should not be understood as "titles". Old master pictures did not have titles and were usually referred to by their subjects. Modern "titles" given to old pictures have no authority. It would be impossible to entitle the present picture without giving a false impression of its subject. Oil painting on oak panel 133 × 115 cm., anonymous [c. 1550?] after Hieronymus Bosch

anatomical knowledge to appreciate it, while a sign-board which has hung outside a pharmacy in all weathers must obviously be read as a shop-sign first and a subject-picture (or whatever is left of one) second. But the converse is also true: identification of the subject can help to guide one towards the name of a painter (as the antiquarian André Féliben was already claiming in the seventeenth century),[4] to suggest an original setting, or to pinpoint a date. For example, the Library has a painting (fig. 3) by a German painter, Adam Elsheimer (1578-1610), who left his native Frankfurt am Main for Italy c. 1598, never to return. The fact that the subject is the beloved German (though Hungarian-born) saint Elizabeth (1207-1231), countess of Thuringia, visiting one of the hospitals which she founded in Eisenach and in Marburg an der Lahn, suggests that the picture was painted before the artist left his native land i.e. before c. 1599, and not for an Italian client in the painter's last decade. Thus a knowledge of iconography contributes to the history of the arts as well as to the history of the subjects depicted.

ICONOGRAPHIC COLLECTIONS

When pictures have been collected or arranged by subject, they constitute an iconographic collection. There have been many iconographic collections in the past, initiated by the fact that many pictures have been brought into being by an interest in their subject and were collected for that reason by their first and subsequent owners. Among early subject collections which have been well studied are the collection formed by Ferdinand Archduke of Tyrol (1529-1595); the print collection which, in the early seventeenth century, was displayed in the anatomy-theatre of Leiden University; the massive collection of engravings gathered by the Abbé Michel de Marolles (1600-1681), which formed the nucleus of the present Cabinet des Estampes in the Bibliothèque Nationale in Paris; and the collection of drawings and prints amassed by the English diarist Samuel Pepys (1633-1703), which still survives at Magdalene College, Cambridge, as a precious example of a systematic, subject-based collection forming an integral part of a distinguished library.[5]

Following this tradition, there are many iconographic collections in existence today, of which some preserve old collections (for example the Département Iconographique of the Bibliothèque Publique et Universitaire in Geneva, which contains items relating to the Reformation, the Genevan Enlightenment and local topography), while others, such as the Iconography Collection of the Harry Ransom Humanities Research

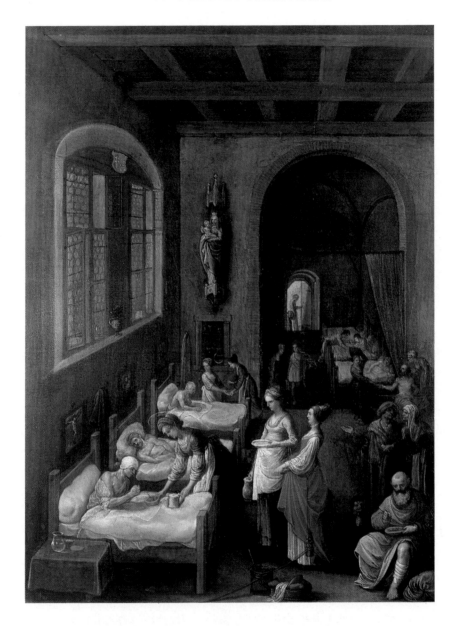

Fig. 3 Saint Elizabeth visiting the sick. She was the daughter of King Andor II of Hungary and wife of Louis, Landgrave of Thuringia. After her husband's death, she gave away her worldly possessions and turned the income from her dowry over to the building and running of a hospital in Marburg, in which she personally cared for the sick, the poor and the homeless—the subject of this picture. Among other details of hospital life, the painter has placed a painting above each of the beds, and despite his sacred theme, has not eschewed such homely details as the slop-bucket in the centre foreground and the slippers and chamber-pot under the bed in the lower left corner. See further p. 54. Oil painting on copper 27 × 19.5 cm. by Adam Elsheimer, Frankfurt am Main [c. 1598?]

Fig. 4 cholera in the Jura, 1854 with Paul-Ferdinand Gachet (seen from behind, right) attending the sick. Wellcome acquired from Gachet's remarkable collection this drawing and those among the other items which were most pertinent to medical history. See further p. 54. Pencil and charcoal with white highlights on paper 31.1 × 46.2 cm. by Amand-Désiré Gautier, Paris 1859

Center, University of Texas, Austin, are new creations. The Wellcome Institute's Iconographic Collections, initiated around 1900, are younger than the former and older than the latter.

Medical iconographic collections have been created by medical men, for example T.J. Pettigrew (1791-1856) in England and Clements C. Fry (1892-1955) in America, but rarely by institutions before the twentieth century, if we exclude medical institutions which have merely grown old in the possession of works of art. The groundwork for institutional collections was laid by men such as the Montpellier professor of physiology Jacques Lordat (1773-1870), who published in 1833 an "essay on medical iconology" inspired by the bequest of the Atger collection of drawings to the library of the Montpellier medical faculty.[6] More specifically, a remarkable sketch for a medico-historical print collection was published in 1861 by Karl Friedrich Heinrich Marx of Göttingen (1796-1877). Marx compiled long lists of prints divided into thirty-five subject-classes covering almost all the subjects which would be represented in the corresponding section of the Wellcome Institute Library over fifty years later.[7]

In the second half of the nineteenth century new institutional collections began to appear, notably in Washington D.C., where the Surgeon-General's Library inaugurated in 1879 what is now the Prints and Photographs Collection of the National Library of Medicine. Many other collections exist today in Europe and America, each possessing its own character. Those in museums tend to emphasize the commemorative nature, and those in libraries the documentary value of their pictures. The Wellcome Institute Library's Iconographic Collections seem to be the major British contribution to this international enterprise.

THE WELLCOME INSTITUTE LIBRARY'S
ICONOGRAPHIC COLLECTIONS

The Iconographic Collections of the Wellcome Institute Library are collections of prints, paintings, watercolours, drawings, photographs and miscellaneous other media. Their countries of origin and the subjects treated in them are substantially the same as for material in other departments of the Library, which means that they come from every continent of the globe and, in subject, refer to the history of the broad mutal influences of sickness and health on the one hand and science, learning, religion, economics and ways of life on the other. Historians, the medical world, publishers, broadcasters and the interested public use the Iconographic Collections for research and educational purposes. Medical lecturers use slides of Wellcome Institute pictures to represent the historical dimension behind current medical topics. Pictures are used in exhibitions both at the Wellcome Institute and at other institutions: in recent years, they have been lent for exhibition in Britain, Belgium, West Germany, Canada and Japan.

history and methodology

Most of the pictures which constitute the collections were acquired by Sir Henry S. Wellcome and his agents between the late 1890s and 1936, the year of Wellcome's death. Wellcome was an American-born pharmaceutical manufacturer who, having emigrated to England and built up his business, acquired an immense number of historical artefacts of all kinds in an attempt to mark out an exhaustive system of medical anthropology on an evolutionary model.[8] In the quest for evidence of unbroken chains of cognitive development, he employed agents in Britain and travellers in Europe and Asia to seek out and acquire books, pictures, instruments, bygones, relics and memorabilia which would present his vision of human history to the public at a specially constructed museum in London. The history of this institution is yet to be written, but a little is known of the purchases which came to form the present Iconographic Collections of the Wellcome Institute Library.

The sources from which Wellcome acquired material were very diverse. His main source of supply was the London auction-houses with their vast turnover of works of art, books, autograph letters and material of "ethnographic" interest brought home by servants of the Empire. It was at one of these auctions, for example, that Wellcome acquired in 1920 the collection of Tibetan paintings and drawings owned by the tibetologist and medical man L.A. Waddell. When a collection of portraits, papers, and personalia of Edward Jenner was offered at Sotheby's on 25-27 November 1918, Wellcome bought every lot.

Fig. 5 Henry S. Wellcome portrayed at the age of fifty-three. In 1895 Wellcome had come into sole possession of the pharmaceutical firm Burroughs Wellcome & Co., and at the time of this portrait was still expanding its range of products and subsidiaries. He was also turning his mind increasingly to patronage of medical research, archaeology, anthropology, philanthropy, and above all collecting. In the remaining thirty years of his life, these activities formed virtually a second career for Wellcome. They offered great scope for the application of his passionate interest in medical history, one of the fruits of which is the present Wellcome Institute Library. Oil painting on canvas 112.5 × 88 cm. by Hugh Goldwin Riviere, London 1906

Some items were volunteered as gifts, many more were bought for small sums from dealers or private collectors. To limit examples to pictures, Wellcome in person bought many in Spain and Portugal, and he closely supervised negotiations with the Roman collector E. Gorga, which finally brought him in 1924 a collection of votive paintings from the church of S. Agostino in Rome. One of his agents, known as Captain Saint (i.e. Peter Johnston-Saint, 1886-1974), scoured the *bouquinistes* on the Left Bank of the Seine for drawings and prints of medical subjects, and thought nothing of sending back to London a seven-foot long predella, painted with scenes in the life of St. Roch, which he discovered for Wellcome in an antique shop in the French Pyrenees.

Wellcome also commissioned pictures. His interest in the cultures of the American and Canadian Indians led to his patronage of artists portraying medicine-men in their traditional costume, "so that", as Wellcome put it, "the pictorial representations will conform as far as possible with their primitive state before their contact with the white races and our so-called civilisation."[9] Contemporary English illustrators such as Francis Barraud (1856-1924) and Ernest Board (1877-1934) were employed to provide paintings of scenes from medical history. For portraits of himself (fig. 5) Wellcome commissioned Hugh Goldwin Riviere (1869-1956) whom he may have come to know through the painter's brother, an eminent physician.

If an original item was unavailable, as in the case of Bosch's so-called "Garden of earthly delights" mentioned on p. 4 above, Wellcome was happy to acquire or commission a copy so that at least the iconography of the original should not be absent from his grand design. The copies have proved useful when the original has vanished (like the Dutch paintings once in Dresden) or decayed (like Sir Joshua Reynolds' portrait of John Hunter).

In choosing acquisitions, Wellcome was generally indifferent to the aesthetic quality and condition of pictures, books and manuscripts. The purpose of his collecting was not to satisfy the desire for beautiful objects, but to provide study-material for the natural and human sciences. As an acquisition, a cosmological diagram in poor condition might be more desirable from this point of view than a fine old master drawing. Hence Wellcome avoided the then fashionable markets for art-collectors, such as early Italian engravings, books of hours or fine etchings in rare states, and concentrated on unloved and offbeat areas where less money could be spent to greater effect, at least in theory. As a result of this policy, the Iconographic (and the other) collections are marked by a haphazard distribution of aesthetic merit which often puzzles art-historians and bibliophiles unfamiliar with Wellcome's taste.

Fig. 6 "Syphilis" by Richard Cooper. A picture commissioned by Wellcome in September 1910: similar pictures commissioned from the same artist between 1909 and 1911 show cholera, diphtheria, typhoid, tuberculosis, cancer, leprosy and plague. They formed a grisly ensemble in Wellcome's first historical venture, his "Historical Medical Museum" exhibited at 54a Wigmore Street, London, in 1913, in conjunction with the XVIIth International Congress of Medicine. Here Cooper, an English illustrator working in Paris, shows, half-realistically, half-allegorically, how an Edwardian sporting man of the world (characterised as such by his golf-clubs, souvenirs of the turf, and signs of good living) reacts to the revelation of his own infection with a then treatable but generally uncurable and horrific disease. Gouache and watercolour on board 52 × 70.5 cm. by Richard T. Cooper, Paris 1910

The core of the present Wellcome Institute Library is composed of the books and pictures originally collected for the purposes of Wellcome's historical museum, the remainder of the museum collections—sculpture, ceramics, instruments, weapons etc.—having been distributed since Wellcome's death to other institutions.[10] Although the essential character of the Wellcome Institute's collections has been determined by Henry Wellcome's interests and decisions, the Institute is no longer bound by its founder's speculative scheme and is free to select from current historical thinking whatever lines of approach allow good use of the existing material.

Now owned and supported by the Wellcome Trust (a British registered charity), the Library has acquired and is still acquiring iconographic material by gift and purchase, though not on the same scale as in the founder's lifetime. Though privately owned, the Library provides a public service, in consideration of which Her Majesty's Government has contributed to the cost of special acquisitions in recent years.

There are certain methodological *caveats* which seem particularly pertinent to the Wellcome Institute's collections, though those who are familiar with subject-collections in other fields might well claim that they are universal. In the first place, researchers who approach this historical pictorial archive from a starting-point in medicine or literary studies should be aware that pictures of medical subjects do not form a straightforward pictorial equivalent to the medical literature of their time (still less of our time). For example, books on consumption are legion but pictures

Fig. 7 Christ healing a leper. The woodcut technique used here produces bold black lines which stand out individually against the white ground. The absence of middle tones produces an intense, simplified vision which, as it happens, is suitable to illustrate the simplicity of the biblical narrative (Matthew VIII, 1-4). Woodcut could not be used to render even the rough lesions of leprosy—supposing that the biblical disease so called was considered in the sixteenth century to be the same as the mycobacterial disease called leprosy today—but, like the biblical text, it renders the social rather than the pathological features of the disease: the leper carries a clapper to warn of his presence, wears a face-mask, and meets Christ outside the city. See further p. 54. Woodcut 10.5 × 14 cm. by an anonymous woodcutter c. 1571 after Jost Amman, Nuremberg

of consumptives are few. The discrepancy occurs partly because a high proportion of medical books has been produced by medical practitioners but the same is not true of pictures of medical subjects, and partly because, just as what writers wrote or did not write was influenced by literary and linguistic traditions, so makers of pictures also have followed a course peculiar to their art. For example Jost Amman's 1571 woodcut of a leper (fig. 7) was derived not from an actual leper but from an engraving made by an earlier print-maker, Virgil Solis, in the late 1550s.[11] Even when not following so closely the internal traditions of their art, artists show a natural bias towards scenes which happen to form lively compositions of figures (such as dentistry and quack-doctors) and away from subjects for which there was no contemporary demand from the picture-buying public. Thus the seeker of a portrait of James Parkinson (the describer of Parkinson's disease) or of an illustration of the "Black Death" made by some phlegmatic eye-witness in 1348 will seek in vain.

Second, the types of pictures which exist from different epochs depend also on what kinds of pictures were allowed by prevailing artistic techniques to come into existence at all: here the internal history of the arts has a direct bearing on the documentation of medical history. For example the sixteenth century was the great age of the woodcut in Europe (fig. 7), but woodcut is a poor technique for the depiction of skin-diseases, an art which only became possible with the establishment of coloured tonal reproduction-techniques in the later eighteenth century: the colour mezzotint, which was used by Jacques-Fabien Gautier d'Agoty to produce the first illustration of what he believed to be penile chancre of syphilis in 1773, and the colour stipple-engraving, which was first used to illustrate a range of skin-diseases by Robert Willan in the 1790s. In the following century, new techniques came and went (inter alia the lithograph, the hand-coloured photograph, the chromolithograph and the half-tone), each endowed with different capacities to render the various aspects of dermatoses. Obstetrical illustration, on the other hand, is a very different story. The linear techniques (drawing, engraving, sculpture) which are used to show the foetus in utero have existed for millennia, and the earliest surviving examples date from the ninth century A.D. (Brussels, Bibliothèque Royale MS 3714). Hence the student of medical history, whether through words or through pictures, needs to keep in mind that to some extent the subject is subordinate to the medium.

Third, pictures, like works of literature, should not be treated as privileged, objective witnesses transcending the ordinary powers of the historical document (which may, however, be considerable). On the contrary, their value lies precisely in the fact that they are locked in their own time and place in history. One feasible form of research is therefore

15

(continued on p. 18)

Figs. 8-11 practitioners of four of the sundry occupations which influence health and   sickness

此中國睹香之闢也病人服藥無效請瞽者
視此項皆係婦女家進假託神鬼言語以促
人聽香燒爐中有之用藥或許愿則癒效否
而可耳

Fig. 8 an "incense-watcher" or superstitious "wise woman" who, judging from what she sees in the flame of the candle, discerns the course of illness, discovers the most suitable time for giving medicines, and foretells other turns of fate

此中國醫道之國也京中醫士有太醫御醫
之稱乃是在太醫院應差者如有人請馬錢
二吊四百文四吊八百不等如來到門首有
病者給錢數百名為門脈

Fig. 9 a physician of the imperial court taking a lady's pulse on an expensive home visit

Watercolours on rice paper c. 26 × 34.4 cm. by Zhou Pei Qun, Beijing, early 19th century

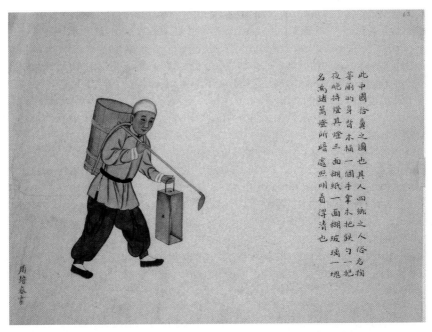

此中國拾糞之圖也其人四鄉之人俗名掏
茅厠的身背木桶一個手拿木把鐵勺一把
夜晚持燈其燈三面糊紙一面糊玻璃一塊
名為糞燈所暗處照明看得清也

Fig. 10 a humble collector of night-soil setting off with his lantern in the very early hours of the morning

此中國串鈴賣藥之圖也其人係江湖之士
微通醫數明點藥性口有俊才即往各省遊
藝手持串鈴搖動有一小方旗上書善治病
症不等看病時目視其色言能變化藉此賣
藥無非求衣食耳

Fig. 11 an itinerant medicine-vendor ringing a finger-bell to draw attention to his arrival. The heading on his placard tells patients to come to his office at "Lu shun tang" (the house in the smooth street). The rest of the text is indicated only schematically but it would typically indicate the range of treatments available (e.g. specialist surgery, acupuncture, herbal therapy). The yellow bag holds his samples of medicines

the comparision of pictures of a given subject with references to the same subject in other contemporary media, such as songs, legal documents or textbooks, which are represented in other departments of the Library. One might ask, for example, how alchemists of the kind shown in paintings by the Flemish painter David Teniers the younger (1610-1690), and reproduced by copyists in innumerable contemporary versions, were related to the contemporary authors and copyists of the arcane alchemical tracts which the Library's department of Western Manuscripts has in profusion. Are the human viscera as depicted in a Nepalese coloured drawing (fig. 12) the same as those described in Sanskrit medical texts? How better to illuminate the business papers of "Sequah", which are in the Library's Contemporary Medical Archives Centre, than by a vivid painting of that late Victorian medical phenomenon, which is in the Iconographic Collections? Such cross-departmental research is the rule rather than the exception. Though housed separately for archival expediency, the Iconographic Collections are not supposed to be intellectually self-sufficient; nor, indeed, is the Institute as a whole.

The prospective researcher in the Wellcome Institute Library should also note that the Library's pictorial resources are not limited to the Iconographic Collections, for a wealth of photographs, drawings and prints is found among the archives, manuscripts and printed books in other departments of the Library. The printed books also include the essential secondary literature on medical iconography to which researchers should refer before they apply to study the primary documents in the Iconographic Collections.* For researchers who do not need to see original items, collections of photographic reproductions are available: these are more convenient for rapid scanning.

Exclusions which will be important to some researchers are that the Iconographic Collections have no original material from ancient Greece, Rome, Egypt, Babylon or Assyria (though they do contain later drawings, prints and photographs copying such material), no mediaeval miniatures, no collection of Jewish pictures and little in the way of arabica. These lacunae appear to result from the non-existence of suitable items. In other fields, material may exist but the Wellcome Institute Library has not been able to collect it; there is nothing from most states of the Soviet Union, for instance. Chronologically there is no cut-off point—the latest material in the collections dates from the 1980s—though some periods are covered only very thinly.

*For preliminary guidance, select lists of some of these source-books, primary and secondary, are given on pp. 59-67 below.

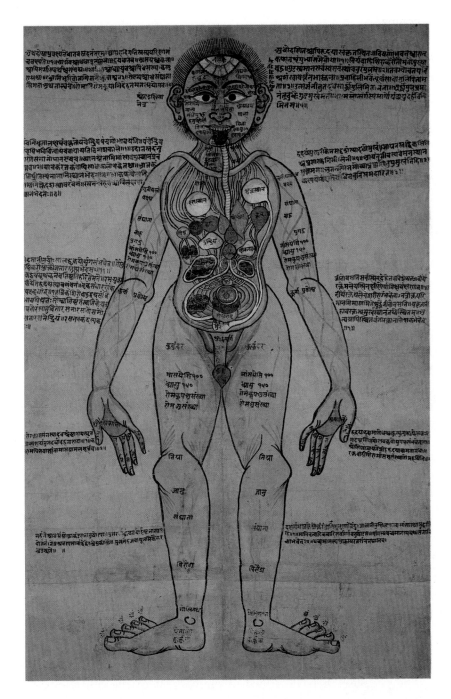

Fig. 12 a male human figure showing parts of the body with texts in Nepalese (written on the body) and Sanskrit (written around the periphery). See further p. 54. Pen and ink, watercolour and gouache on paper 62.5 × 40.5 cm., anonymous, Nepal [c. 1800?]

The foregoing might give the impression that the Iconographic Collections are more restricted than some readers would hope, but in certain respects they have a broader range than many would expect. They include, for instance, pictures of town and country, customs and manners, cults, occupations and entertainments—not exclusively "medical" subjects. The reason for their presence in the Library is that Wellcome was naturally inclined to follow the instruction of the first Hippocratic aphorism, that the medical man should consider not only the patient and his attendants but also "things from outside". This required him to take into account the larger spheres of nature and society which encircle and press on the minutiae determining the changing balance of health and sickness in the individual person. For example, a single patient with a fever exists in several environments: the vegetable, which provides febrifuges such as quinine; the intellectual, which nourishes the bio-medical sciences; the spiritual, which affects the patient's attitude to his illness; the material, in the form of sanitary conditions; the microbiological, which may have precipitated the fever; the economic, which determines the grade of medical attention the patient can afford; and the demographic, which distinguishes isolated cases from epidemics and pandemics. In order to discover the patient's place in history, the enquirer must explore these and innumerable other environments through their surviving documents, including iconography, which in this example may range among botanical illustration, views of laboratories, devotional prints and paintings, antiquarian sketchbooks and any other genres which might be relevant.

Turning from the patient to the doctor, the researcher will find that the actions of medical practitioners in the past must be approached from an equal variety of viewpoints, for even the core of medicine, the clinical care of patients, has often consisted of a few extremely simple acts which in turn rest on a variety of scientific, cultural, social and religious assumptions. For example a sound historical interpretation of the commonplace act of taking the pulse (fig. 9) may force the (sometimes reluctant) researcher to enquire into the history of anatomy, musical notation, pneumatology, and professionalisation, which subjects are therefore considered as being conjugate with the history of medicine. The Library as a whole, and the Iconographic Collections as a department of it, reflect these ramifications of the subject, even though, given the breadth of the existing collections, current acquisitions are chosen to support the trunk rather than the branches.

The pluralism here described in the content of the collections is matched in the ways in which they are used. Despite their name, they are not reserved exclusively for iconographers but are also available for any other form of historical argument. They even have their uses for nonhistorical ends, since many subjects of medical iconography are still familiar today, such as the doctor redoubling his dogmatism when he has run out of knowledge; the patient's confusion at conflicting diagnoses; the admired man of science, commemorated by his portrait; and the inevitability of death.

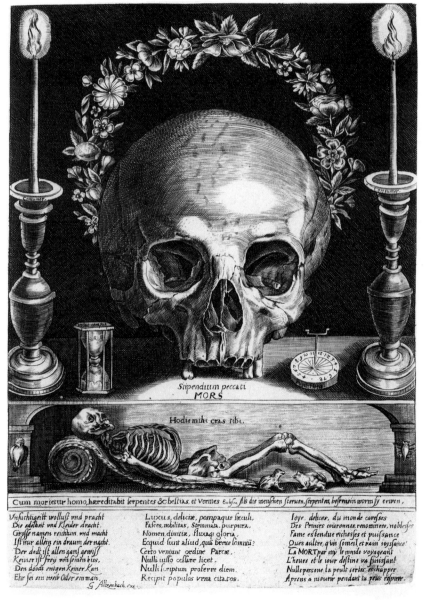

Fig. 13 a reminder of the limits of life. See further p. 55. Engraving 28.5 × 20.5 cm. by Gerhard Altzenbach, Cologne [c. 1660?]

The following notes give brief information about the Iconographic Collections according to the principal divisions in which they are currently arranged, and explain some of the terms used to describe different kinds of pictures.

drawings and prints

The Library has a large collection of original prints. Their number has proved difficult to estimate and is in any case of no significance in itself, but it is certainly in excess of 50,000. The collection has not yet attained a steady state, for many prints and some drawings are still being accessioned, much has still to be done in the way of organization, and new acquisitions on a smaller scale continue to improve the stock.

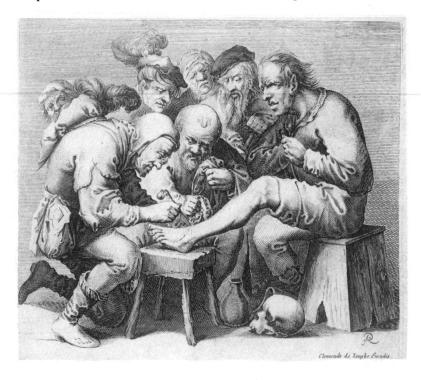

Fig. 14 a minor surgical operation. The engraving technique, here used sparingly, produces lines which, in combination, can show middle tones, and therefore a more unified atmosphere, better than woodcut (fig. 7) but not as well as the lithograph (fig. 18). The operator is of the low, itinerant kind, as is suggested by his plumed hat which was worn to gain attention in public squares. At the end of his lancet is probably a bladder-stone which he has extracted from an earlier customer. As this was not offered as a technical illustration, the nature of the operation is not shown. Instead the artist concentrates on the distracted state of the patient and the attentiveness of the onlookers. Engraving 19.5 × 22.4 cm. by Pieter Jansz. Quast (Amsterdam 1606-1647)

Prints come in many varieties. *Line-engravings* are printed from a plate (usually a sheet of copper) in which grooves have been cut and inked to print black on those areas of the paper where lines are required for the design. Dark areas are represented by cross-hatching or by close parallel strokes, all cut laboriously into the plate (fig. 14). An *etching* is a kind of engraving in which areas which are to print black on the paper are not cut by hand but are bitten out of the copper plate by the application of acid. Areas of the plate which are to leave the paper unmarked are protected from the acid by a waxen coating (fig. 15). As a consequence of their respective techniques, line-engravings tend to have regular and repeated lines whereas etchings show a more free and cursive ductus.

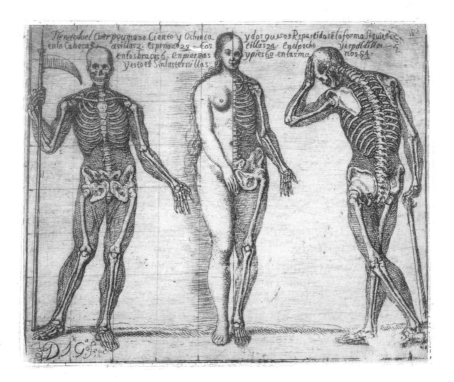

Fig. 15 three human figures showing the bones. An example of an etching. The designer and etcher was José García Hidalgo, a painter in the service of kings Charles II and Philip V of Spain. He was advisor on paintings to the Spanish Inquisition, and was described by a contemporary as "of strange and extravagant temper" (Zahira Veliz, Artists' techniques in golden age Spain, Cambridge 1987, p. 129). He produced this etching to instruct painters in anatomy, knowledge of which was essential to the figure-painter. A later draftsman has drawn a grid of squares over the left figure to guide him in copying it: this addition shows that the plate fulfilled its purpose. Etching 16.6 × 20.3 cm. by José García Hidalgo (1656-1718), Madrid

Fig. 16 a gin-shop in London in the mid-eighteenth century. The dark ground of the mezzotint is ideal for suggesting the sinister gloom of the evil boding London gin-shop. See further p. 55. Mezzotint 25 × 35.5 cm. by an unknown draftsman and engraver, published in London by Carington Bowles [c. 1770?]

Another kind of engraving is the *mezzotint,* which is produced by selective smoothing-down of the burr on a roughly ploughed-up copper plate. When inked and printed, the misty greys of the half-smoothed parts of the plate give a heroic atmosphere to portraits of men of action such as surgeons and hospital-founders; darker grounds from rougher plates envelop thoughtful physicians in the gloomy twilight of their studies; and the inky blackness of the hispid areas produces wonderfully eerie night-scenes (fig. 16).

The techniques mentioned above are called "intaglio" (cut) processes, meaning that the design is translated into inked furrows or shallows cut out from the surface of the plate, while the smooth swathes of uncut copper are wiped clean of ink and therefore leave the paper white after printing. Engravers often employed a mixture of intaglio methods on one plate, for example combining line-engraving and etching. There are numerous other kinds of intaglio print, including *stipple, aquatint, dry-point, crayon-manner* etc., most of which are represented in the Wellcome collections.

Woodcut, on the other hand, uses the opposite method, called "relief": using a stout wood-block instead of a thin copper-plate as the printing piece, the woodcutter gouges out of the surface of the block all the parts which are to appear as white on the paper, thus leaving standing out, in the form of wooden ridges, the lines and smooth areas of wood which, when inked and pressed against paper, print in black or colours (fig. 7). To produce colour woodcuts, unless the paper is to be tinted by hand, several blocks are cut, each one for a different colour of ink (fig. 17). The fact that, in a woodcut, the design is created by the residue of *subtraction* of matter from the block rather than by any kind of positive intervention, fascinated the mind of the seventeenth-century virtuoso trained in Aristotelian metaphysics: in John Evelyn's words, "(by a seeming paradox) as the *Matter* diminishes, the *Forme* increases, as one wastes, the other growes perfect."[12] (The paradox is sharpened by the fact that the Greek word for matter, $\overset{c\prime}{\upsilon}\lambda\eta$, also means wood.)

Fig. 17 Westerners taking tea at Yokohama. A colour woodcut showing the effect obtained when several different woodblocks are cut, each one for printing in a different colour of ink. See further p. 55. Woodcut printed in colours 35.6 × 48 cm. by Yoshikazu, Tokyo 1860, signed in left and right margins; panels at foot of design include the mark of the block-cutter Chikahisa

Unlike the techniques just described, *lithographs* are made not by cutting the design on a plate or block but by drawing it in a greasy medium on a very smooth surface (originally stone, later zinc). The greasy areas are inked and the design transferred from them to the paper which is pressed against the stone. Lithographs are recognized by their soft, non-linear tonal character (fig. 18).

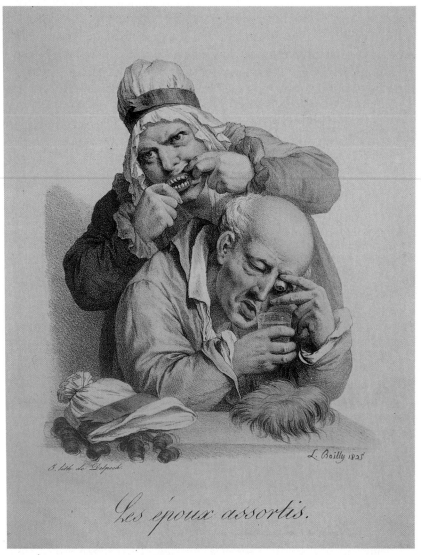

Fig. 18 a lithograph, distinguishable from an intaglio print by its soft application of continuous tone on a smooth surface. See further p. 55. Lithograph 25 × 20 cm. (subject) by Louis-Léopold Boilly, published in Paris as part of a collection of "Grimaces" by the widow Delpech, 19 February 1825

Fig. 19 a quack-doctor and his assistant drawing a crowd at a country fair. See further pp. 55-56. Pen and ink and watercolour 13.6 × 16.2 cm. by Thomas Rowlandson (1756-1827)

Drawings, watercolours, gouaches etc. are made by such numerous different combinations of techniques that it is not possible to describe them here. Examples are shown in the frontispiece and fig. 19. Among the watercolours, Asian items probably outnumber European examples in the collection (e.g. figs. 8-12 above).

The most accessible part of the collection is available in the Print Room in the Wellcome Institute Library. All the prints are delicate, many of them are rare and most are not yet mounted or otherwise protected for safe handling: consequently, they are not on open access but are, as in most print rooms, available to *bona fide* researchers by appointment with the curators. The same applies to other works on paper (drawings, watercolours, pouncings etc.), which, by comparison with the prints, are quite few in number. Drawings and prints are not placed on permanent exhibition owing to the harmful effects of light and atmosphere on paper and pigments, but some are usually on temporary display in the Institute.

Some of the subjects covered by the prints, drawings and watercolours will be seen from a brief survey of selected classes in the present state of the classification scheme. The scheme is literally provisional in the sense that it provides places for the material and has no claim to philosophical status like the abstract classifications of Dewey and Bliss. Items are housed in solanders in alphabetical order of the classes printed in **bold** type below, but because prints of different sizes within each class must be stored in different places, the class-names are not necessarily a guide to the physical arrangement of the material. Neither this classification scheme nor any other could be an adequate substitute for a good subject index, but such an index cannot be compiled until the physical organisation of the pictures allows it. In the absence of an index, the curators will gladly advise researchers on the whereabouts of suitable materials insofar as they are known.

1. MEDICINE AND SURGERY

In this section is found the history of clinical medicine and medical knowledge *as it appears in drawings and prints.* This last qualification will explain the absence of many aspects of clinical medicine (orthopaedics, radiology etc.) which have not been treated in these media, either because they are of specialist interest or because they are relatively recent arrivals in the medical world.

Firstly there are members of the medical professions, seen with or without their patients. **Apothecaries** are shown making up and dispensing medicinal substances, at first as solitary pharmacists in their shops, sometimes with the assistance of a boy, and later replaced by the staff of laboratories and large factories. **Physicians and surgeons,** excluding portraits which form a class of their own, include character-types, costume-studies, illustrations of myths and literature, and works of art which, for whatever reason, show medical practitioners at work or at leisure. Many healers have been abused as quacks, but since a certain amount of white-lying is unavoidable in medicine, **quacks** are here strictly defined as mountebanks, people who use a variety of traditional patters to sell medicines in a public place. Their theatrical performances have endeared them to connoisseurs of low life, including many artists (fig. 19).

Lay-people are found in the role of patients in prints of **nursing,** not only by professional nurses in their relatively brief history as a profession but also by religious, relatives of the sick and domestic servants. **Diseases** shows cities—Rome, London, Marseilles—convulsed by the bubonic plague, the disease which has left the most durable impression on European culture; there are also a few items each on smallpox (fig. 20),

Fig. 20 Tametomo repelling the smallpox from the island of Oshima. For the story see p. 56. Woodcut printed in colours 35.5 × 24.5 cm. by Utagawa Yoshikazu, dated from the two censorship seals 1847/1852

cholera, goitre, leprosy and syphilis. A class of **abnormalities** includes dwarfs, "spotted boys" (negroes with partial albinism), "fasting girls", transvestites and long-lived persons. Patients also appear in so many other classes that the classification would collapse if they were given a class of their own.

Dentistry for example represents experiences familiar to artists in the role of patient and perhaps for that reason depicted with special feeling. The operators come in all types: the blacksmith, the itinerant expert, the routine tooth-drawer and those more polite, more pretentious, figures of the eighteenth century who added prosthesis to their repertoire (cf. fig. 18) and who called themselves "dentistes" in an attempt to raise up something like the modern dental profession. **Naval and military medicine and surgery** includes a substantial amount of material on the Crimean War and the role of Florence Nightingale (1820-1910). In many prints she was depicted as "The Lady with the Lamp", but holding, instead of the historically correct Victorian lantern, a well-trimmed antique oil-lamp of the kind depicted in the hands of the wise virgins in the parable (*Matthew* chapter 25). This fanciful stereotype persists in Florence Nightingale's portrait on the present British ten pound bank-note which is based on prints in the Wellcome collection: it has probably helped to perpetuate an image of the ever-attentive nurse. Most pictures in this class are more severe, however. From the First World War they include five large drawings by Austin Osman Spare (1886-1956), who combined cultivation of the occult with the duties of a War Artist in the Royal Army Medical Corps. From the Second World War comes a group of watercolours by Leo Rawlings, made in Changi prison camp, Singapore, during the Japanese occupation.

Among other aspects of practice, **surgery** records the many minor operations which formed the day-to-day work of a surgeon (fig. 14), and a few major operations (lithotomy, mastectomy, amputation of limbs). Pictures of specific surgeons at work are elaborately staged set-pieces which are classed among **group-portraits. Therapy** includes all other forms of intervention, such as inoculation against rabies, serum-therapy for diphtheria, resuscitation of the drowned, water-therapy in every imaginable form, electrical therapy for the exhausted debauchee, and unspecified medicinal draughts. "What to do before the doctor comes", a pair of Turkish lithographic broadsheets issued by the Ottoman Red Crescent organisation *c.* 1900, each measuring 81 × 111 cm., is probably the largest item among the prints in this class: this, if any, is a typical Wellcome *trouvaille*. There are also small groups of prints dealing with **hygiene, ophthalmology,** and **veterinary medicine.**

Institutions account for a large collection of prints and drawings of hospitals, alms-houses, educational establishments, health resorts, halls of colleges etc., housed in alphabetical order of place-name. Institutions in London are further classified according to their location in *old* (pre-1963) boroughs (e.g. St Pancras, Hampstead, Holborn etc., rather than Camden), since this is the classification used in public health literature and statistics of the time.

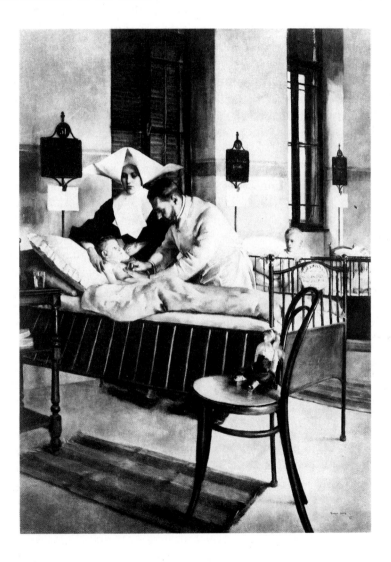

Fig. 21 "Im Kinderspital" ("In the children's hospital"). On the subject see p. 56. Heliogravure 55.7 × 40.4 cm. by F. Löwy, Vienna 1901, after Imre Knopp, Budapest 1892

Two classes which are not subject-classes at all but *genres* have grown up more by popular demand than through their suitability for the classification: **caricatures** and **allegories.** The collection of English caricatures forms a fine and precious resource, and there are smaller collections of their Dutch, French, German, Italian and American equivalents. The French caricatures include many satires on the use of the clyster and on vaccination against smallpox. Since caricatures are hard to define, they will also be found in other classes, particularly **dentistry.** **Allegories** illustrate the five senses, the four temperaments, the stages of life, medicine, the sciences, etc.

Of the old medical sciences—institutes of medicine, therapeutics, forensic medicine etc.—only **anatomy** has left a substantial iconography (*materia medica* is subsumed under **botany** in the next section). The earlier items in this class include a red chalk drawing attributed to Michelangelo (fig. 22). In a later century the surgeon and neuro-anatomist Sir Charles Bell (1774-1842) looked back to Michelangelo as "the true painter-anatomist", but Bell himself was also a fine artist and art-teacher, his teaching being revealed in a series of impressive chalk-drawings made in his London anatomy-school in 1815 by one of his pupils, Charles Landseer, who was then only sixteen years old. Anatomical prints made in the intervening three centuries include engravings by Philips Galle of Antwerp (1537-1612), three etchings by José García Hidalgo of Madrid (1656-1718) (fig. 15), colour mezzotints by Jacques-Fabien Gautier d'Agoty (*c.* 1717-*c.* 1785), and many book-illustrations for the instruction of medical students. Some of the prints are yellowed by daylight, stained with old varnish, or perforated with the stigmata of frame-tacks around the edges, evidence that they were once hung up as a teaching-aid in some foetid dissecting-room of a previous century. Some dissecting-rooms of this type are shown in prints of **anatomical dissections**, which also include material on the related activity of grave-robbing.

Sub-classes of anatomy include **morbid anatomy**, today generally called pathology, which includes what appears to be the publisher's stock of coloured plates for Richard Bright's *Reports of medical cases,* London 1827-1831, including the classic description of the kidney-disease named after him. Other sub-classes are **phrenology; physiognomy;** and **reproductive anatomy**, mostly engraved book-illustrations published for students of midwifery.

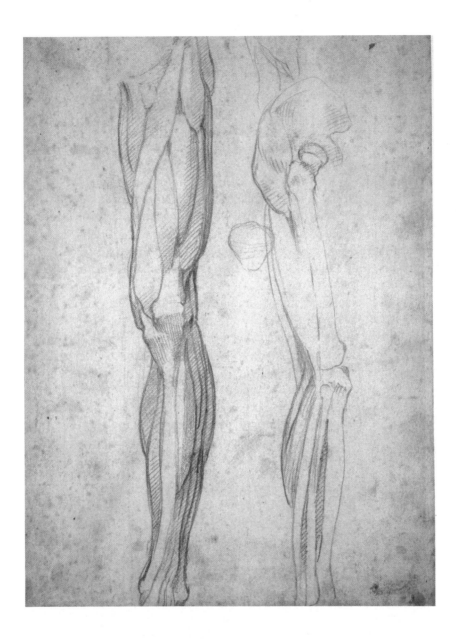

Fig. 22 muscles and bones of the lower limb. See further p. 56. Red chalk on paper 27.8 × 20.3 cm. attributed to Michelangelo Buonarroti (1475-1564) c. 1505/1520. Purchased for the Wellcome Institute Library in 1982 and presented in memory of the medical historian Dr Robert Heller (1907-1980) and Mrs Anne Heller

2. SACRED SUBJECTS

When sacred subjects have played an important part in people's healthy lives, they will *a fortiori* have been essential to their experience of illness and death, and therefore cannot be ignored by even the least religious-minded of modern medical historians. Their iconography is extremely rich: pictures of gods, holy families, saints, avatars, *mūrtis* and *lohans* received projections of their worshipers' hopes and aspirations for lives free from trouble (including disease). Illustrations of sacred books and myths include acts of healing which have a venerable place in medical mythology: the subjects which William Hogarth painted on the staircase walls of Saint Bartholomew's Hospital, London, in 1735-1737—the miraculous cure at the pool of Bethesda (*John* chapter 5) and the charity of the good Samaritan (*Luke* chapter 10)—had been used for centuries as exemplars for patients and patrons of hospitals and almshouses. Many of these subjects are represented by prints in this department of the Library. Another kind of print is the *santino* or small, often hand-coloured, devotional print of a saint: Wellcome amassed these popular ephemera in Spain, Italy, Austria and France, and they are now housed together with fine prints of the same subjects to give a rounded iconography of saints who were often a first and a last resort in illnesses and other crises. The fact that they are housed in subject-order rather than by school or artist should make this part of the collection a useful resource not only for medical history but for all branches of history which take account of hagiography. From the Buddhist world there is an important collection of Tibetan bodycolour drawings and paintings on paper and cloth: their intricate iconography is unravelled in a catalogue which is in an advanced state of preparation.

3. SCIENCES

Medicine, though not itself a science, absorbs nutriment from many sciences, whose histories are therefore duly documented in the Wellcome Institute Library. Prints in the Iconographic Collections show, at a general level, scientific lectures, meetings, demonstrations, the public face of the sciences, as well as individuals wrestling with scientific problems. More particularly, **alchemy and chemistry** are represented by prints of laboratories, equipment, and those who used them. A large collection of prints and drawings illustrates the various divisions of natural history, including **botany** and **geology.** Many of the prints of these subjects are small engravings from books, but the opportunity for artists to depict such paragons of the 'sublime' as rainbows, volcanoes and geysers has also left some splendid watercolours and gouaches in the Wellcome collections. Among the quantitative sciences, **astrology, astronomy,** and

Fig. 23 Saint Valentine, bishop of Terni in the third century, depicted in this Polish
print as "patron of serious disease": the legend probably alludes to epilepsy, the saint's
patronage of which appears to be due to the assonance between Valentine and the
Germanic names for epilepsy, Fallsucht, fallende Sucht, or falling sickness. The
"falling" position of the man at the saint's feet is meant as the attribute of the epileptic.
Hand-coloured engraving 20.1 × 16.2 cm., anonymous, Poland [c. 1800?]

metrology are represented. There are also collections dealing with the useful arts, nowadays called technology, though this modern term seems less appropriate for such traditional skills as bee-keeping, farriery, and the cooling of drinks.

Fig. 24 the "hall of natural philosophy" in the building of the Felix Meritis society, Amsterdan, the audience attending a demonstration of electrical generation by Jan Hendrik Van Swinden (1746-1823), who is seen from behind on the right of the table. Van Swinden was a versatile man of science—meteorologist, author of Mémoires sur l'analogie de l' électricité et du magnétisme *(1784), and especially popularizer of the physical sciences. The society, a forum for amateurs of the arts and sciences, existed from 1777 to 1888 at 324 Keisersgracht, Amsterdam, a building which has more recently served as headquarters of the Dutch Communist Party.* Engraving 44.5 × 55.2 cm. by Reinier Vinkeles after a drawing by two hands: the figures by Jacques Kuyper, the remainder by Pieter Barbiers, Amsterdam [c. 1800?]

4. SOCIAL SUBJECTS

Fig 25 a picture of people—a family of pea-shellers—in the context of their working lives. See further p. 56. Engraving 42.1 × 47.6 cm. by Jacques-Philippe Le Bas, Paris 1760, after J.-B. Greuze, c. 1755/1759

Since the section called medicine and surgery (pp. 28-33 above) embraced only the history of clinical medicine and medical knowledge, many aspects of the history of medicine which are represented in popular prints are excluded from it. The use of **alcohol** and **narcotics** does not usually require the presence or knowledge of a physician but merely a suitable social ambience (fig. 16). Such subjects are therefore included in the large section called social subjects. The classes mentioned above include the series of prints, entitled *The Bottle,* made by George Cruikshank in the temperance cause in 1847, and a pair of Chinese paintings on rice-paper showing the decline of an opium-smoker from prosperity to destitution. Other elements in society which might have attracted medical expertise but did not necessarily do so include children; the lame, handicapped or crippled; the famished; the poor; slaves; prisoners; animals; and the dead, who were of course capable of infecting all the others if not properly treated. These are represented in prints and drawings, as are their converse: foundling hospitals; the supply of food, housing and clothes; bathing and drainage; burial and cremation; and other services which have gathered around the old "Seven works of mercy" of frequent depiction. Subjects more intimate to the person, but nevertheless much represented in prints, include **toilet, ablutions, coiffure** and **dress,** containing collections of prints satirising such dangerous vanities as tight corsetry and high hair-pieces. Other classes bearing on ways of life include **transport, working-conditions,** and **family relationships.** A collection of prints on **murder, massacre and torture** (including self-inflicted) has its uses for researchers studying the history of pain: it results from Wellcome's specification in 1905 that "curious methods of torture and execution" be included in his collection.

This very brief review of social subjects omits much that might be included, but at present the collection awaits further organization. However, the class of **topography** must be mentioned for it contains large collections which the medical historian could easily overlook. Let one little watercolour (fig. 26) stand for hundreds of items.

Fig. 26 the quarantine station on St John's Island, near Singapore, 14 June 1879. See further p. 57. Watercolour on paper 17.3 × 24.5 cm. by J.F. Taylor, Singapore 1879

Fig. 27 Carl Friedrich Wilhelm Ludwig (1816-1895), physiologist. See p. 57. Lithograph 25.6 × 20.8 cm. by Rudolf Hoffmann, 1856, after a photograph by Ferdinand von Küss, Vienna

5. PORTRAITS

Drawings and prints containing **portraits** of individual practitioners of medicine, surgery, the sciences and related professions have been arranged in alphabetical order and catalogued. There are also collections of **personalia** such as illustrations of an eminent person's birthplace or tomb. Some **group-portraits** have also been organised for use, but many others await curatorial attention. Portraits include a set of drawings made by one Carlo Ernesto Liverati (1805-1844) of members of the third *Riunione di scienzati italiani* in Florence in September 1841: among the Italian scientists one is surprised to find a portrait of the English mathematician Charles Babbage F.R.S. (1792-1871). The prints include extensive holdings of engraved and lithographic portraits of German and Austrian sitters. Perusing the catalogue is a fascinating pastime as one discovers such rarities as a lithographic portrait of Dr Joseph McCarogher, physician to the Chichester Infirmary in the early nineteenth century, beneath whose bust appears a street-accident in which the artist, Filippo Pistrucci, was run over (Dr McCarogher set and cured his broken leg).

There are typescript lists of the drawings and prints in some of these classes, e.g. **alcohol, anatomy, apothecaries,** and there is a published catalogue of individual portraits (see p. 60). However, since the classes themselves are still not adequately defined, and further large accessions from uncatalogued reserves are calling for the creation of new classes, it will be many years before adequate catalogues of the entire collection can be published. The size of the collection can be indicated by the fact that, of the sixty subsections mentioned above, the largest class, *individual portraits,* contains not less than 15,000 items, and a smaller class such as *anatomy,* holds about 1,500 items (drawings, watercolours and prints only).

paintings

The oil paintings in the Wellcome Institute Library are peculiarly heterogeneous when considered from the art-historical point of view, but are coherent as a collection of materials on their subject. While the collection includes a few pictures by masters who are considered important in the history of artistic styles (for example Adam Elsheimer, Benjamin West, Joseph-Marie Vien), that is not the prime purpose of the collection, and many more pictures are the work of traditionalist, amateur or provincial practitioners. 'Naive' art, which is also represented, has its own principles (Legibility before Virtuosity), and its examples are all the more valuable since so many have unfortunately been destroyed through a failure to appreciate their historical interest. Most of the paintings are of course on panel or canvas; others are on copper, tin, iron, zinc, cloth, marble, millboard, paper, porcelain and glass. There are works in many genres, from the altarpiece to the shop-sign, dating from every century since the fifteenth, and originating from most countries of Europe. Being fewer than the prints, they cannot be divided so easily into large subject-classes, and are therefore considered here by their countries of origin.

Wellcome's collecting expeditions in Spain brought him several fine **Spanish** panel-paintings of the early sixteenth century, notably a painting of saints Cosmas and Damian transplanting the leg of a Moor on to the thigh of a Christian verger, as a miracle rather than as a routine operation (fig 28). Later Spanish paintings in the collection are almost all votive pictures: one of them, dated 1770, commemorates the recovery from fever

Fig. 28 Saints Cosmas and Damian performing a miraculous feat of surgery: amputating the ulcerated leg of a Christian and transplanting in its place the undiseased leg of a dead Moor. See further pp. 57-58. This painting is the largest, most finely worked, and best preserved of the earlier pictures in the collection, and Wellcome spared no efforts to obtain it. Oil painting on panel 168 × 133 cm. attributed to Alonso de Sedano, Burgos, c. 1495

of the son of a medical doctor (Manuel Estevan Perez de los Rios, son of Juan Manuel Perez M.D.).

Recent years have seen a great increase in publications on the iconography of **Dutch** paintings of the seventeenth century, and in the stream of this interest much attention has been given to works of this school in the Wellcome Institute Library. One feature of the collection is the presence of more than one painting by a single artist: thus, though their names will be familiar only to connoisseurs of Dutch painting, there are two paintings of surgical scenes by Gerrit Lundens of Amsterdam (1622-1683); two if not three paintings by Hendrik Heerschop of Haarlem (1620-after 1672), one of an alchemist, the others of uroscopy; at least three paintings of alchemists and philosophers by Thomas Wijck of Haarlem, London and elsewhere (*c.* 1616-1677); and no fewer than five by Matthijs Naiveu (1647-1721), painter of Amsterdam voluptuaries enjoying the fruits of empire (and needing medical attention as a result). It is a curious fact that although all four of these painters are represented in the Rijksmuseum, Amsterdam, none of them (at the time of writing) has any paintings in the National Gallery, London, and the same is true for two other painters who are represented each by one large painting in the Wellcome Institute: Pieter de Grebber of Haarlem (*c.* 1600-1652/3) and Joost-Cornelis Droochsloot of Utrecht (1586-1666). The Wellcome Institute has by the former a depiction of a rare patristic subject, Herodias mutilating the tongue of the Baptist, and by the latter a painting of the halt and the blind being summoned to the rich man's feast (*Matthew* chapter 22, *Luke* chapter 14), in which one of the guests is portrayed as the painter himself.

Among the **Flemish** paintings there is a dramatic illustration of a surgical emergency by Jan-Joseph Horemans the elder of Antwerp (1682-1759), and several paintings by and after the poorly documented and today often confused painters Gerard Thomas and Balthazar van der Bossche, who both worked in Antwerp in the late seventeenth and early eighteenth centuries. The once great popularity of their paintings of alchemists, physicians and philosophers remains to be explained.

Apart from a few earlier works, the **Italian** pictures include a score or more of votive paintings from the eighteenth and nineteenth centuries, including many which depict and once hung around Jacopo Sansovino's sculpture known as the Madonna del Parto (1518) in the church of Sant' Agostino in Rome. Other were collected in Sicily, Tuscany and elsewhere.

Devotional paintings of a different kind were also collected in **Greece** and **Turkey**: these are representations of medical saints (Cosmas, Damian, Pantaleon etc.), of the Byzantine legend of the Fountain of Life, and of miraculous cures.

Fig. 29 the "Fountain of life". On the subject see p. 58. Central part of a gilded and painted triptych 65.5 × 34.4 cm. with two wings (not shown in the photograph) 41 × 17.4 cm., each painted inside with eight figures of saints, anonymous, Greece, date unknown

The **British** paintings almost defy generalization. One may however say that they are all (so far as known) of secular subjects. A number of them are dental scenes in the style of John Collier ("Tim Bobbin", 1708-1786), meaning that they are grotesques of the most savage kind, and an interesting guide to a certain eighteenth-century sensibility. The Victorian paintings are dominated by a vast canvas showing a garden-party given by the wealthy philanthropist Baroness Burdett-Coutts to members of the International Medical Congress in London in 1881: signed "A. P. Tilt" and dated 1882, it is believed to have been painted by three brothers with the same initials, who all died of tuberculosis shortly after completing their *magnum opus.* This seems a sadly inappropriate end, for the Congress which they commemorated was most significant for diffusing knowledge of the new science of bacteriology to the physicians and surgeons who came from all over the world to attend it.

The most remarkable **French** paintings are the series of twelve life-size depictions of skeletons and muscle-figures painted on canvas in the style of the mezzotint-artists Jacques-Fabien and Arnauld-Eloi Gautier d'Agoty in the eighteenth century. Also on an anatomical theme is a large canvas by Emile-Edouard Mouchy (1802-*c.* 1870?) depicting a physiology lesson in which a dog is vivisected (fig. 30). It dates from the period (1832) when François Magendie was bringing this method of research to the attention of the medical world. Apart from a few paintings of sacred subjects—notably a predella with scenes in the life of Saint Roch, painted *c.* 1620 and purchased in the Pyrenees—most of the other French paintings in the collection are portraits. One of the finest is a portrait of the surgeon Jean-Zuléma Amussat (1796-1856), one of the pioneers of the colostomy, painted in 1846 by Jean-Guillaume-Elzidor Naigeon (1797-1867). Amussat's papers are also in the Library (Dept. of Western MSS). More recent medical men portrayed include, among Wellcome's illustrious contemporaries, the medical physicist Jacques-Arsène d'Arsonval (1851-1940), the physiologist Charles-Robert Richet (1850-1935), and the microbiologist and clinician Jean-Hyachinthe Vincent (1862-1950).

A mass of other items in this collection includes portraits and devotional paintings from the German states, apothecaries' sign-boards from Austria and Ireland, topographical pictures from India and Canada, and a painting of the black Virgin of Guadalupe painted in 1743 at Her shrine near Mexico City.

Sorting and cataloguing of the collection is still in an early stage and it is impossible to say precisely how many paintings it contains, though there are certainly at least 500 items. An annotated subject-catalogue is

Fig. 30 a physiology lesson in Paris in 1832. See further p. 58. Oil painting on canvas 112 × 143 cm. by Emile-Edouard Mouchy, signed and dated 1832

in course of preparation. A *Provisional author-handlist*, which is available for consultation at the Enquiry Desk in the Library, lists at present about 450 paintings: many more remain to be listed.

Like the prints and the rare books, the paintings are kept as a study-collection. They are therefore stored on closed access, but are available for consultation by appointment. A selection of them is exhibited in the Institute's public rooms and galleries. The curators can give advice about uncatalogued paintings and about others which are in storage.

photographs

Photography was a special interest of Sir Henry Wellcome. One reason for this was perhaps the fact that the development of the art of photography owes much to the efforts of medical men in the mid-nineteenth century such as Hugh Welch Diamond and Etienne-Jules Marey, photographs by whom are in the collection. As a direct result of Wellcome's awareness the Library has some of the earliest photomicrographs (by Léon Foucault and Alfred Donné, *c.* 1860), and, among clinical material, a large collection of photographs of people with nervous and orthopaedic disorders, made by L. Haase in Berlin during the 1860s. The Roentgen-Schuster collection, recently presented, includes a set of the earliest x-ray photographs made by Wilhelm Konrad Roentgen in his laboratory at Würzburg in December 1895. Patients at Friern Hospital (formerly Colney Hatch lunatic asylum) in north London are recorded in an unpleasant photograph album compiled before the First World War by one of the physicians at the asylum, who also collected photographs of the brains of deceased patients. On a lighter note, there is, among the many photographs of South Africa, an album of over 200 photographs of the British Association for the Advancement of Science's meeting in Cape Town in 1905; the subjects include Groote Schuur hospital and the photographers include the physicist Sir William Crookes (1832-1919).

Photographs of social subjects include the glass negatives made by John Thomson in the 1860s and 70s to illustrate the people, customs and topography of China and Indo-China (unfortunately none of Thomson's prints seems to be in the collection). Admirers of Sir Patrick Manson

Fig. 31 the notice by the door reads "DR SMITH SURGEON". The location of Dr Smith's dilapidated surgery is not indicated but the presence of another impression of this photograph in an Australian collection suggests Australia: see P.J. Phillips, Kill or cure? Lotions, potions, characters and quacks of early Australia, Adelaide 1978, p. 17. Photographic albumen print 9.5 × 15.4 cm. by Washbourne [c. 1880]

F.R.S. (1844-1922), the discoverer of the aetiology of filariasis, are interested to see, among Thomson's beautiful landscapes, photographs of Amoy, where Manson carried out his research from 1871 to 1883. Photographs of Middle Eastern subjects are to some extent documented in Gillian Grant's *Middle Eastern photographic collections in the United Kingdom* (Oxford 1989).

There is a collection of about fifty moving films including both modern works on the history of medicine and old historic documents. Of the latter class, one shows amputation of the leg in Berlin in 1900, and another the typical activities of the British and Chinese staff of the Henry Lester Institute of Medical Research, Shanghai, in the 1930s, including the Director taking afternoon tea at 4.25 p.m. The collection includes cinematic, videotape and videocassette films.

Handlists of the Thomson photographs and of some of the other photographs are available in typescript, but much curatorial work has yet to be done on works in this most recent of the media in the collections. Eventually the Wellcome collection of photographs will doubtless be the exclusive subject of a booklet such as the present one. What is known of the collection at present suggests that it contains many rare items. Two are illustrated here (figs. 31, 32).

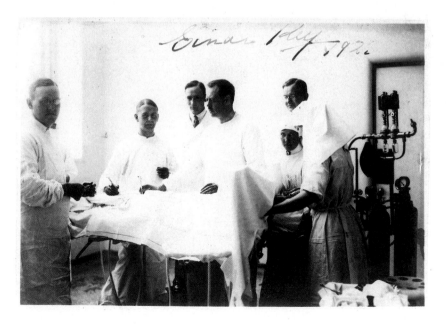

Fig. 32 Einar Key (fourth from left) in the operating theatre. See further p. 58. Photographic print 10.6 × 15.6 cm., anonymous, Sweden, date unknown

In addition to photographs in the strict sense (negatives and prints), there are numerous collections, large and small, of items produced by photomechanical printing methods such as photogravures, half-tones etc. They include a collection of portrait-cuttings amassed by the medical historian Isidor Fischer (1868-1943) in Vienna, and Sir Henry Wellcome's collection of postcards (fig. 33). These materials, derivative though they may be, are in many cases the only surviving records of their subjects.

LOUISE MALONEY HOSPITAL, KEY WEST, FLA.

Fig. 33 postcards such as this souvenir of the "Louise Maloney Hospital, Key West, Florida" were produced to be sent by patients and by their visitors to friends and relatives. (For German examples see A.H. Murken, Hier liegt mein Mann und lässt schön grüssen. Das Krankenhaus auf alten Postkarten, *Münster 1978.) The garish colouring was supposed to give a cheerful impression.* Photomechanical reproduction of a hand-coloured photograph 8.9 × 14.1 cm., anonymous, published by Frank Johnson, Key West, Florida [c. 1930?]

conclusion

This archive is undoubtedly one of the richest of its type in the world. But, despite the devoted work of previous curators, it is still not easy to use. The fact that it is arranged iconographically should ease the path of the researcher, but in practice the arrangement has prolonged the task of sorting and delayed the production of catalogues: the individual portrait-prints took twenty-three years for identifying the sitters and arranging the prints in alphabetical order (1935-1957) and then another ten years (1964-1973) to catalogue. The subjects of many of the items are difficult to interpret, and unlike printed books, most old pictures do not have authentic titles. The collection is large in bulk and its physical arrangement is exceedingly complex. Two cognate pictures cannot be housed together if their surface areas differ in size by a factor of 2000. Many of the pictures are repulsive if not regarded with an historian's eye, while some of the more alluring may be the least historic. Since much of the material is fragile, severe restrictions have to be placed on the handling of original documents.

Fortunately there is also much to be said of a more encouraging kind. Though conservation problems are formidable, they are not unique to this collection, and they are receiving the attention of conservation teams expert in postponing the effects of time on oil-paintings and works on paper. The possibility of translating pictures into numbers by electronic means and then back again into pictures may eventually make stock control, identification, communication and retrieval of pictures much easier and quicker than at present. The use which writers and readers have already made of them, whether by original research or through published reproductions, testifies to the value of the sound pictorial documentation which the Wellcome Institute Library's Iconographic Collections can afford to the explorer in the many fields which they cover. The future work of scholars and curators will continue to exploit and enrich them.

REFERENCES

1. For a lucid introduction see Roelof van Straten, *Een inleiding in de iconografie: enige theoretische en praktische kennis,* Muiderberg, North Holland, 1985. Some material from this book was presented in English in *artibus et historiae* (Venice), 1986, **13**: 165-181.

2. Aelian, *Varia historia* 10.10, *cf.* Aristotle, *Topica* 140 a 18-22 and Pliny, *Naturalis historia* 35.5.16 (the latter referring to portraits inscribed with the names of the sitters). Aelian's story assumes that alphabetic writing preceded painting but of course painting, and pictographic scripts, came first.

3. E. H. Gombrich, *Aby Warburg: an intellectual biography,* 2nd ed., London 1986; William S. Heckscher, 'The genesis of iconology' in his *Art and literature: studies in relationship,* edited by Egon Verheyen, Baden-Baden 1985 (*Studia spiritalia* vol. 17), pp. 253-280. Jane Kromm, 'Hogarth's madmen', *Journal of the Warburg and Courtauld Institutes,* 1985, **48**: 238-242.

4. Jan Bialostocki, 'Iconography', *Dictionary of the history of ideas,* vol. 2, New York 1973, pp. 524-541, quotation on p. 534.

5. The history of earlier subject-collections of graphic works would merit further research. Its neglect is due to the former monopoly of the aesthetic approach among historians of the arts, which Wellcome (among others) was content to sidestep. The following literature may be found useful for its bearing on the subject: Peter W. Parshall, 'The print collection of Ferdinand, Archduke of Tyrol', *Jahrbuch der kunsthistorischen Sammlungen in Wien,* 1982, **78** (n. F. XLII): 139-184; T.H. Lunsingh Scheurleer, 'Un amphithéâtre d'anatomie moralisé' in *Leiden University in the seventeenth century,* edited by T.H. Lunsingh Scheurleer and G.M.H. Posthumus Meyjes, Leiden 1975, pp. 216-277; W.W. Robinson, ' "This passion for prints": collecting and connoisseurship in northern Europe during the seventeenth century', in *Printmaking in the age of Rembrandt,* ed. Clifford Ackley, Boston 1981, pp. xxvii-xlviii and 308-315; Jan van der Waals, 'The print collection of Samuel Pepys', *Print Quarterly,* 1984, **1**: 236-257; Michael Bury, 'The taste for prints in Italy to *c.* 1600', *Print Quarterly,* 1985, **2**: 12-26; Wolfgang Krönig, *Il Duomo di Monreale e l'architettura normanna in Sicilia,* Palermo 1965, pp. 260-262; G.W. Leibniz, quoted by Adolf von Harnack, *Geschichte der königlich preussischen Akademie der Wissenschaften,* Berlin 1900, vol. 2, pp. 78-81; Rudolf E.O. Ekkart, 'Collections of portraits in Western Europe', in Royal College of Physicians of London, *Portraits,* vol. 2, Amsterdam 1977, pp. 1-23; Noë Legrand and Louis Landouzy, *Les collections artistiques de la Faculté de Médecine de Paris,* Paris 1911, pp. 37-39; Duncan Macmillan, *The Torrie collection,* Edinburgh 1983; André Masson, *The pictorial catalogue. Mural decoration in libraries,* Oxford 1981.

6. Jacques Lordat, *Essai sur l'iconologie médicale ou sur les rapports d'utilité entre l'art du dessin et l'étude de la médecine,* Montpellier 1833.

REFERENCES

7. Karl Friedrich Heinrich Marx, 'Uber die Beziehungen der darstellenden Kunst zur Heilkunst', *Abhandlungen der Königlichen Gesellschaft der Wissenschaften zu Göttingen,* 1861-2, **10**: 1-74. After three chapters of introduction, Marx lists prints in the following sections:

    4. the physician with a urine-flask
    5. scenes showing confidence in the physician (Alexander the Great and Philip of Acarnania; the Goltzius series of prints)
    6. the physician at the bedside
    7. the physician at study; consultations of physicians; apothecaries
    8. surgeons, barbers, dentists
    9. charlatans
    10. cripples, patients
    11. care of the sick, works of mercy, the good Samaritan
    12. healing, miracle cures
    13. prophylaxis: vaccination, temperance (and drunkenness)
    14. therapeutics: bathing, laughter, optimism
    15. healing fountains, spas
    16. sex and fertility
    17. pregnancy
    18. childbirth, swaddling
    19. teratology
    20. the ages of man; old age
    21. the five senses
    22. the temperaments
    23. misfortunes and massacres
    24. sleep
    25. dreams
    26. sleeplessness, sleepwalking, nightmares
    27. fainting; recovery from apparent death
    28. suffering, pain, martyrdom, wounding, circumcision, flaying of Marsyas etc.
    29. burning; being struck by lightning
    30. blindness; dumbness
    31. drowning, starvation, exposure
    32. poisoning
    33. mental disorders: possession, hallucination, witches, melancholy, fools, etc.
    34. malaria, cholera
    35. lameness, gout
    36. leprosy, syphilis
    37. typhus, plague
    38. death.

8. Wellcome never set out explicitly the principles of his collecting but they have been skilfully reconstructed by Ghislaine M. Skinner, 'Sir Henry Wellcome's museum for the science of history', *Medical History,* 1986, **30**: 383-418.

9. H.S. Wellcome, letter of 25 July 1931 to the artist, W. Langdon Kihn (Wellcome Institute Archives). The Wellcome Institute Library has seventeen pastels made by Kihn as a result of Wellcome's patronage.

10. Georgina Russell, *Museums Journal*, 1986, **86:** supplement. The Wellcome Museum of the History of Medicine, in the Science Museum, South Kensington, London, holds the biggest portion of Wellcome's museum-collections.

11. Ilse O'Dell Franke, *Kupferstiche und Radierungen aus der Werkstatt des Virgil Solis,* Wiesbaden 1977, no. b 66 and p. 69.

12. John Evelyn, *Sculptura,* London 1662, p. 56.

Fig. 34 The protection of historical documents from the effects of Time is the foremost task of the Library. Even now, some documents, notably those which are longer than 120 cm., have to be rolled or folded and stored like the documents in this print. Etching 9.2 × 18.8 cm. by Louis du Guernier the younger (Paris 1677—London 1716)

NOTES ON THE ILLUSTRATIONS

Fig. 1 The Liverpool School was founded after the Rt. Hon. Joseph Chamberlain, Secretary of State for the Colonies, invited the General Medical Council and the medical schools to make provision for teaching tropical medicine to doctors serving the needs of the British Empire in the tropics.

The figure on the right who looks into the microscope is Professor (later Sir) Rubert William Boyce (1863-1911): he was the first Holt Professor of Pathology at University College, Liverpool, and first Dean of the School of Tropical Medicine. Behind him is Charles Scott Sherrington (1857-1952), who had been Holt Professor of Physiology at Liverpool since 1895. C.S. Sherrington (later Sir Charles) became celebrated for his work on the nervous system—he introduced the term "synapse" to describe the junction between nerve cells—but he also included tropical medicine and medical history among his many interests. While at Liverpool Sherrington published, together with Boyce and Sir Ronald Ross, a paper 'on the history of the discovery of trypanosomes in man (*Lancet,* 1903, i: 509-512). The third author of this paper, Ross, may be the figure on the left of the drawing. Having achieved great fame for his discovery of the means of transmission of malaria, Ross was appointed first Lecturer in Tropical Diseases at the School and, in 1903, Alfred Jones Professor of Tropical Medicine, a post which he held until 1912.

The present gouache was reproduced as a wood-engraving and published in *The graphic* on 17 June 1899, p. 765, with the legend "Professor Boyce and Professor Sherrington examining malarial microbes". The original drawings for illustrations in *The graphic* were available for sale at a special gallery run by the journal at 195 Strand; probably Wellcome sent someone to buy the original gouache of this illustration at the time of its publication.

Fig. 2 Apart from Bosch's autograph version of his composition, three sixteenth-century copies are recorded, the other two in Paris and Madrid. The Wellcome copy was catalogued by Gerd Unverfehrt, *Hieronymus Bosch: die Rezeption seiner Kunst im frühen 16. Jahrhundert,* Berlin 1980, as no. 161c. Sir Henry Wellcome bought it at auction in 1931, when it was sold from the estate of an English collector, W.M. Newton.

The subject of the picture is problematic, but most scholars interpret it as a hostile view of the life devoted to the pleasure of the senses. The first author to leave a specific description of Bosch's composition, Fray José de Sigüença, referred to it in 1605 as "el quadro del madroño" (the picture of the strawberry), interpreting the gigantic strawberry near the centre as a typically transient object of the senses of smell and taste. E.H. Gombrich has refined this interpretation by suggesting that the people depicted are intended to be those who lived before the Flood: among other reasons for this identification, a popular mediaeval text, the *Historia scholastica* of Peter Comestor (twelfth century) states that the earth was less fertile after the Flood than before, when fruit and flowers had grown to enormous sizes (as in Bosch's picture) and mankind had been vegetarian (E.H. Gombrich, 'Bosch's "Garden of earthly delights": a progress report', *Journal of the Warburg and Courtauld Institutes,* 1969, *32:* 162-170). Other interpretations have found alchemical, astrological or millenarian lore in the picture, while yet others localize it in a feature of Bosch's time, the outburst of moralistic mockery of the self-indulgent mob. See Paul Vandenbroeck, *Jheronimus Bosch: tussen volksleven en stadscultuur,* Berchem 1987.

Fig. 3 The painting is in Elsheimer's early style, painted probably at the age of about twenty, while he was still in his native city of Frankfurt am Main. The figures bear some resemblance to those found in the art of the *Dürerzeit*. While the picture was in Germany its authorship was recognized, for example when it was auctioned by Lempertz in Cologne, 1 December 1927. In England, however, Elsheimer's name conjures up the paintings which he produced in a more articulate, baroque style during his later years in Italy: after the Wellcome painting passed to England, unfamiliarity with his German paintings led to neglect of its traditional attribution until it was re-asserted by Krämer in 1978 (article cited on p. 60 below). See also Keith Andrews, 'Once more Elsheimer', *The Burlington Magazine,* 1979, *121*: 168-172; Axel Hinrich Murken and Burkhard Hofmann, 'Die Heilige Elisabeth als Krankenpflegerin', *Historia hospitalium,* 1979-1980, *13*: 7-28; Keith Andrews, *Adam Elsheimer,* 2nd edition (first German-language edition), Munich 1985, pp. 14, 174. The painting has been exhibited not only at the Wellcome Institute but also in Frankfurt am Main and in Marburg, where its presence contributed in 1983 to the 700th anniversary celebrations of the Elisabethkirche: see Brigitte Rechberg, *Die Heilige Elisabeth in der Kunst: Abbild, Vorbild, Wunschbild,* Marburg/Lahn 1983, no. 55.

Fig. 4 On the right, identifiable from his distinctive shock of (actually red) hair is Paul-Ferdinand Gachet (1828-1909), here a young medical student, but later well-known both as a Paris physician specializing in unorthodox treatments (electrotherapy, homoeopathy, psychosomatic therapy) and, under the pseudonym Paul van Ryssel (i.e. Paul of Lille, after his birthplace), as a painter and printmaker. Bored by his medical studies in Paris, Gachet had jumped at the opportunity to help care for the isolated cholera patients in the Jura in the epidemic of August 1854. Kneeling on the left is his companion, the artist Amand-Désiré Gautier, who made this drawing in 1859 from earlier sketches, and also a painting, now lost (P. Gachet, *Deux amis des impressionistes: le docteur Gachet et Murer,* Paris 1956).

The drawing formed part of Gachet's collection, which had been enriched by his acquaintance with an extraordinary number of artists and writers, from Daumier and Hugo in an earlier generation to Cézanne and Van Gogh, both of whom he taught to etch while they stayed in his home-village of Auvers-sur-Oise. Wellcome acquired in 1927 from Gachet's son those items of his collection which had a bearing on medical history, including Van Gogh's etched portrait of Gachet *père,* the present drawing, and drawings which Gachet had collected by insane patients at the Salpêtrière hospital.

Fig. 7 The print was designed by Jost Amman (Zürich 1539-1591) for his *Icones novi testamenti,* Frankfurt am Main 1571. Catalogued by C. Becker, *Jobst Amman,* Leipzig 1854, as no. 1.h.5, and by A. Andresen, *Der deutsche peintre-graveur,* vol. 1, Leipzig 1864, as no. 184.5.

Fig. 12 Whereas the Sanskrit medical tradition is profusely represented in written texts, this diagrammatic drawing appears to be uncommon if not unique in being a pictorial statement of the "anatomical" and "physiological" principles embodied in those texts. A thorough analysis of this document—no easy task in view of its complexity—has yet to be carried out.

Fig. 13 a compendium of death-motifs with verses in German, Latin and French. "The pleasures of the world, status symbols, riches, what are they but a brief dream? Learn to die while you can breathe!" The legend *consumor* engraved around the candle-sticks illustrates a paradox familiar in the seventeenth century: the candle is saved at the expense of its purpose, and only redeems itself by self-destruction in a good cause. The comparison was referred to by John Donne (*The canonisation* v. 21), "We are tapers too that at our own cost die".

Fig. 16 The circumstances which gave rise to this picture of a London gin-shop have been described by M. Dorothy George in her classic *London life in the XVIIIth century,* 2nd edition, London 1930, pp. 27-42. The "orgy of spirit-drinking" which was at its worst from 1720 to 1751 was responsible for an alarming lessening of births and increase of deaths in London, though immigration contrived to keep up the numbers. The weakness of the city's capacity for renewal was all the more remarkable because it was a period of prosperity for many and luxury for some. Despite Acts of Parliament passed in 1743 and 1751, it was still said of the gin-shop keepers in 1776 that "these shop-keepers are the principal officers of the king of terrors and have conveyed more to the regions of death than the sword or the plague." As with many impressions of mezzotints published by the house of Carington Bowles, the date of publication, which was originally printed after the publisher's address at the foot of the print, has been almost entirely erased in order to disguise the fading of its topicality. It probably dates from the 1770s but may have been designed earlier.

Fig. 17 After 1853, when Japan was opened up to foreigners, the strange appearance and customs of the latter provoked artists to provide pictures of them for the Japanese market. This picture of what was presumably the western counterpart to the Japanese tea ceremony was made in Tokyo in 1860. In the background, western ships approach the new harbour of Yokohama, bringing changes which would affect all aspects of Japanese life in the Meiji era, including medical science and, to a lesser extent, practice. The same ships would carry woodcuts in this well-developed Japanese style back to Europe where it would also leave its mark in the cult of *japonaiserie.*

Fig. 18 The subject of this lithograph is the indignity of prosthesis, the dark side of the technical improvements which had been made in this field. Like most satires it only shows one side of its subject; other genres, such as advertisements, were available to show the other side. The artist, Louis-Leopold Boilly (1761-1845), includes wigs among the artificial vanities, but when he had started his career as a portrait-painter in the 1780s most of his sitters wore wigs as a matter of course, a fact which indicates the power of convention. The print was catalogued by Henri Harrisse, *L.-L. Boilly,* Paris 1898, as no. 1318.

Fig. 19 A book could be made of Rowlandson's caricatures of the medical world, which cover almost every stage of life (from *A midwife going to a labour* to *The English dance of death*) and every medical rôle (the physician, the surgeon, the apothecary, the nurse and many varieties of patient). The present drawing celebrates the irregular itinerant practitioners who set up in country fairs or city squares, claimed outlandish origins and remarkable cures, and provided more in entertainment than they lacked in straightforward therapy. Although they used traditional methods (for example the zany, on the left of the drawing, derived from the *commedia dell'arte*), their trade was given a fillip by the increasing commercialization of medicine in eighteenth-century England. The notice on the left describes the performer as "The great Doctor Humbugallo, seventh son of a seventh son, healer of mankind and philosopher, cures all infirmities". Seventh sons were alleged to be natural healers (Wayland D. Hand, *Magical medicine,* Berkeley, California, 1980, pp. 45-46; Roy Porter, *Health for sale,* Manchester 1989, pp. 64, 112).

Fig. 20 Chinsei Hachiro Tametomo was a powerful historical figure of the twelfth century A.D. to whom many legendary feats were attributed. His political enemies cut the sinews of his arms to end his skill in archery and exiled him to the island of Oshima in the west of Japan. There, according to legend, he repelled the demon of smallpox who was preparing to enter the island: in response to his ferocious threats, the demon, on the left of the picture, is said to have shrunk to the size of a pea and floated out to sea. The story reflects the wishful thinking of the smallpox-ravaged centuries before the disease was finally eradicated in the late 1970s with the aid of Jennerian vaccination.

Fig. 21 The physician percusses the chest of a child. This method of distinguishing thoracic conditions was the first of a battery of new diagnostic techniques to be added to those handed down in the ancient Hippocratic *corpus*: it was first described by the Viennese Joseph Leopold Auenbrugger in 1761, though—like many new techniques—its potential was not fully appreciated until after its inventor's death. Compared with the hospital depicted in Elsheimer's picture three centuries earlier (fig. 3, p. 7 above), the present picture shows a bleaker room with uglier furnishings: the paintings above the bed have been replaced by a number-sign with a clip for medical records, while the Hungarian notice at the foot of the bed seems to be an official notice of ownership. The comparison illustrates the truism that improvements in medical science and medical care do not always walk in step.

Fig. 22 One in a series of drawings, the others being at Windsor and in the Teylers Museum, Haarlem, one of which is inscribed with Italian verses in Michelangelo's hand, a fact which suggests his authorship of the drawings. It dates from a period when empirical knowledge of human anatomy was sought more for artistic than for medical purposes. On the attribution see E. Schilling and A. Blunt, *The German drawings in the collection of H.M. the Queen at Windsor Castle . . . and supplements to the catalogues of Italian and French drawings,* London [1971], pp. 99-100.

Fig 25 Family size, social stratification, conditions of work, the extent of child labour, and the quality of buildings are among the social factors which are of special interest to medical historians. Pictures of such subjects often represent them in significant ways. In this example a print showing a family of pea-shellers in picturesque poverty is dedicated by the French royal engraver to a banker, M. Jean-Pierre Kolly. The picture was designed in the Flemish manner by Jean-Baptiste Greuze (1725-1805) but the whereabouts of his original painting was not known to J. Martin, who compiled a *catalogue raisonné* of his works (in C. Mauclair, *Jean-Baptiste Greuze,* Paris n.d., where the picture is listed without location as no. 134). Martin identified the two women in the centre as grand-daughter and grand-mother, and the man on the left as the grand-father, leaving the two figures on the right as presumably the grand-parents' daughter looking after their grandson.

Fig. 26 A watercolour by a colonial civil servant who seems to have drawn it as a souvenir of a successful boar-hunt which he enjoyed on the depicted peninsula, with no inkling of the fact that his work would one day be preserved in a medical history library. He pasted it in an album of watercolours and photographs made and collected by him in the Malay Archipelago between 1879 and 1881 (this watercolour is on fol. 11). The building shown in the picture awaits its historian—who should be pleased to find this watercolour to add a touch of vividness to his narrative.

Fig. 27 The existence of Ludwig's portrait in the Wellcome Institute Library acknowledges his important research in the 1840s and 50s on fundamental physiological questions (the mechanisms determining blood-pressure, respiratory exchange, renal secretion, the innervation of glands etc.), the nicety of his experimental technique, his contribution to the development of physiological instruments (notably "Ludwig's kymograph" for measuring *and* recording blood-pressure), his creation of the physiological institute at Leipzig in 1865, and his influence on the students from many lands who attended his lectures there and took his teachings back to their own countries where they contributed to the formation of national schools of physiology.

The common but misguided assumption that 'mere' portraits are all the same and therefore of no interest is surely refuted by the present lithograph—not every physiologist has a duelling-scar on his upper lip.

Fig. 28 Saints Cosmas and Damian practised medicine and surgery without payment according to their legend, and were therefore represented to the lay public as medical ideals. In this Spanish altarpiece they are shown in the full finery of academic doctors as they perform their miraculous operation. The painter shows only one bone running through the limb below the knee-joint, whereas empirical research reveals that there are two, the tibia and fibula. This not uncommon fallacy may be derived from the fact that in classical antiquity the same word *(tibia)* was used for both the larger bone in the leg and for the leg as a whole. The transmission of anatomical knowledge from classical antiquity through the middle ages was almost entirely by written, not pictorial means, as a result of which many terminological confusions came to haunt anatomical beliefs in the fifteenth century. Michelangelo's drawing of the bones and muscles of the lower limb (fig. 22, p. 33 above) is a perfect example of the way in which such confusions were dissolved in the sixteenth century by increasingly sophisticated anatomical illustrations founded on empirical study. Of course empirical study in this context means anatomical dissection, which has not always been socially acceptable. It could be done by an artist in Florence in the early sixteenth century but was not necessarily either available or of interest to an experienced painter in Burgos, northern Spain, at the same time.

For a survey of the iconography of the miracle see E. Rinaldi, 'The first homoplastic limb transplant according to the legend of saint Cosmas and saint Damian', *Italian Journal of Orthopedics and Traumatology,* 1987, *13*(3): 393-406. Cf. Douglas B. Price, 'Miraculous restoration of lost body parts: relationship to the phantom limb phenomenon and to limb-burial superstition and practices', in *American folk medicine* ed. W.D. Hand, Berkeley, California, 1976, pp. 49-71.

On the attribution of the Wellcome painting to Alonso de Sedano see Chandler Rathfon Post, *A history of Spanish painting,* Cambridge, Mass., vol. 4, part ii (1933), pp. 202-210; vol. 5 (1934), pp. 326-331; vol. 9 (1947), pp. 800-803. The attribution rested initially on the stylistic resemblance between the Wellcome picture, an altarpiece of Saint Sebastian in the cathedral of Palma de Mallorca (documented as painted by Pedro Terrenchs and Alonso de Sedano *c.* 1486/1496); and a six-panel altar-piece from Burgos cathedral now in the Diocesan Museum, Burgos. Post was later provided with a document which showed that the Burgos cathedral panels were painted by Alonso de Sedano before 8 July 1496, and which therefore provided a name for the painter of the Wellcome picture also. The latter was probably painted for the church of SS. Cosme y Damián, Burgos, where a copy of this painting was noted by Post.

Fig. 29 The iconography of the fountain of life has been elucidated by Talbot (article cited on p. 61 below). It weaves together three strands: the belief in the existence (somewhere) of a real fountain of youth, a belief which contributed to the use of baths, the development of watering-places etc.; the Christian idea of the fountain of Life, particularly in the phrase "life-giving fountain" (zōodochos pēgē) applied to the Virgin; and the story of the fountain of Balukli near Constantinople, as told by the fourteenth-century historian Nicephorus Callistus, *Ecclesiasticae historiae,* XV, cap. xxv. The soldier who became the Emperor Leo I (ruled 457-474), asked by a blind man to fetch him some water, had a vision which guided him to the spring at Balukli, instructed him to build a shrine there, and told him of his future accession to the imperial throne. After the water cured the old man's blindness, many other cures were accomplished there, which are rehearsed in the liturgy for the Dormition of the Virgin and the Zōodochos Pēgē: these cures are illustrated in the present icon. Leo and the blind man are in the bottom right corner, the other foreground figures included a paralytic and a lunatic, and a schematic view of Constantinople is shown in the background. The Virgin addresses Leo through a ray of Greek text stretching down from the top centre. On the carved head-piece the Holy Trinity is depicted.

Fig. 30 The painting shows a relatively primitive stage in the history of experimental physiology, marked by the absence of anaesthesia for the animals and the crude way in which the dog is restrained. Several groups of young physiologists existed at the time the picture was painted, but attempts to identify this scene have not so far been convincing. For further information see the paper by Schupbach (1987) cited on p. 60 below.

Fig. 32 Einar Samuel Henrik Key (Stockholm 1872-1954) was one of the leading surgeons of his time. Professor of surgery at the Karolinska Institutet, Stockholm, from 1923 to 1937, he devoted himself above all to perfecting the surgical removal of embolisms from the peripheral arteries, an operation which, under his influence, became a local speciality: in 1929 Key wrote that this operation had been performed 216 times and that in 65-70% of the cases the operators had been Scandinavian surgeons. The present photograph, showing the team still without face-masks, was signed by Key in 1923 and presented to an English surgeon, G. Grey Turner, who presented it in turn to the Wellcome Institute Library in 1960.

GUIDES TO LITERATURE

The following guides to literature are in three parts:

(a) literature specifically on items in the Iconographic Collections, Wellcome Institute Library;
(b) secondary literature in which the historical iconography of given subjects is usefully discussed or reproduced;
(c) historic primary works including mainly original iconography in their illustrations.

The lists are *not exhaustive bibliographies of their respective subjects but merely starting-points for research.* An inclusion is not to be interpreted as an endorsement, nor an omission as a slight. If a given subject is not mentioned, it may be either because the compiler has not come across any significant book specifically on the iconography of the subject, or because no such book exists, or because the subject appears to have no significant historical iconography. Manuscript books are not included, nor are books on the iconography of sacred, scientific or social subjects (e.g. saints, zoology, child-rearing) whose essential relation to medicine varies from case to case. The subject-headings used do not imply that research should or even can be divided accordingly, but they may be useful points of reference for those whose studies are comprehensive within a given period or region or are otherwise differently defined.

Most but not all of the books and articles listed are among the printed books in the Wellcome Institute Library. Unbound plates of some of the primary books listed in section (c) are in the Iconographic Collections.

(a) the Wellcome Iconographic Collections

There is currently no unified catalogue or handlist of the Iconographic Collections. The catalogues and handlists of *Wellcome exhibitions* include many paintings, prints and photographs. The inaugural publication was called *Handbook of the historical medical museum organised by Henry S. Wellcome* (London 1913); others have been devoted to Joseph Lister (1927), cinchona (1930), Henry Hill Hickman (1930), Edward Jenner (1949), Chinese medicine (1966), the history of cardiology (1970), German prints (1982), *Morbid cravings: the emergence of addiction* (1984), *Body and mind in Tibetan medicine* (1986); *A vision of history: the Wellcome Institute for the History of Medicine* (1986-1987); *No laughing matter: historical aspects of anaesthesia* (1987).

For *portrait-prints and -drawings* of individual medical and scientific practitioners see the printed catalogue by Renate Burgess, *Portraits of doctors and scientists in the Wellcome Institute,* London: Wellcome Institute, 1973.

Numerous papers illustrate and discuss *individual items in the collection:* the following is a selection.

Renate Burgess, 'Humphry Davy or Friedrich Accum: a question of identification', *Medical History,* 1972, **16**: 290-293

— 'Thomas Garvine—Ayrshire surgeon active in Russia and China', *Medical History,* 1975, **19**: 91-94

— 'Notes on some plague paintings', *Medical History,* 1976, **20**: 422-428

— 'A satire on the influenza of 1803', *Medical History,* 1979, **23**: 469-473

— 'The dance of death', *Society for the social History of Medicine, Bulletin,* 1980, **26**: 25-37

— 'A portrait by Wright of Derby', *The Burlington Magazine,* 1982, **124**: 155-157

Gode Krämer, 'Ein wiedergefundenes Bild aus der Frühzeit Elsheimers', *Pantheon,* 1978, **36**: 319-326

Gertrude M. Prescott, 'Gachet and Johnston-Saint: the provenance of Van Gogh's *L'homme à la pipe*', *Medical History,* 1987, **31**: 217-224

Alex Sakula, 'Baroness Burdett-Coutts' garden party: the International Medical Congress, London, 1881', *Medical History,* 1982, **26**: 183-190

William Schupbach, 'A new look at the cure of folly', *Medical History,* 1978, **22**: 267-281

— 'The fame and notoriety of Dr John Huxham', *Medical History,* 1981, **25**: 415-421

— 'The last moments of H.R.H. the Prince Consort', *Medical History,* 1982, **26**: 321-324

— 'John Monro M.D. and Charles James Fox', *Medical History,* 1983, **27**: 80-83

— 'Iconography of Dr William Kitchiner (1775?-1827)', *Medical History,* 1984, **28**: 202-209

— 'Scriptorium: Wellcome library', *Kos,* 1984, **1** (6): 9-17

— 'Sequah: an English "American medicine"-man in 1890', *Medical History,* 1985, **29**: 272-317

— 'Earl's Court House from John Hunter to Robert Gardiner Hill', *Medical History,* 1986, **30**: 351-356

— 'A select iconography of animal experiment', in N. Rupke (ed.), *Vivisection in historical perspective,* London 1987 pp. 354-374 and 209-213

Enid M. Slatter, 'A note on the botanical prints and drawings', *Medical History,* 1982, **26:** 453-455

Charles Talbot, 'The fountain of life: a Greek version', *Bulletin of the History of Medicine,* 1957, **31:** 2-16

Marianne Winder, 'Il Buddha della medicina', *Kos,* 1984, **1** (3): 55-74

Eric Young, 'Early Spanish panel-paintings in English collections', *Apollo,* August 1979, **110:** 102-107

(b) a select list of (mostly illustrated) secondary literature on the history of medical iconography

GENERAL

For clinical subjects after the Middle Ages the best starting-point is Helmut Vogt, *Das Bild des Kranken,* Munich 1969 (second impression Munich 1980), which has well-organized bibliographies. Illustrated general histories of medicine include: Maxime Paul Marie Laignel-Lavastine (ed.), *Histoire générale de la médecine,* Paris 1936-1949; Pedro Laín Entralgo and others, *Historia universal de la medicina,* Barcelona 1972-1975; Albert S. Lyons and R.J. Petrucelli, *Medicine, an illustrated history,* New York 1978; Jean-Charles Sournia and others, *Illustrierte Geschichte der Medizin* (German translation of French edition, Paris 1978), Salzburg 1980-1984; Heinz Goerke, *Arzt und Heilkunde,* Munich 1984.

Wellcome Institute for the History of Medicine, *Subject catalogue of the history of medicine and related sciences,* Munich 1980, has a range wider than its title suggests, since it is a bibliography rather than a catalogue and includes other related subjects as well as sciences. It differentiates literature on medical subjects in works of art, distinguishes works which are illustrated, and specifies when they are illustrated with portraits.

ABNORMALITIES

George M. Gould and W.L. Pyle, *Anomalies and curiosities of medicine,* Philadelphia and London 1901; Eugen Holländer, *Wunder, Wundergeburt und Wundergestalt in Einblattdrucken des 15.-18. Jahrhunderts,* second edition, Stuttgart 1922

ALCHEMY

Christopher R. Hill, 'The iconography of the laboratory', *Ambix,* 1975, **22:** 102-110; A.A.A.M. Brinkman, *De alchemist in de prentkunst,* Amsterdam 1982   **alchemical imagery** Barbara Obrist, *Les débuts de l'imagerie alchimique (XIVe-XVe siècles),* Paris 1982

ANAESTHESIA

Barbara Duncum, *The development of inhalation anaesthesia . . . 1846-1900,* London 1947; W.D.A. Smith, *Under the influence,* London 1982

ANATOMICAL DISSECTION

Gerhard Wolf-Heidegger and Anna Maria Cetto, *Die anatomische Sektion in bildlicher Darstellung,* Basel 1967

ANATOMY AND PHYSIOLOGY

Johann Ludwig Choulant, *History and bibliography of anatomic illustration,* Chicago 1920 (enlarged translation by Mortimer Frank of the German edition, Leipzig 1852); Loris Premuda, *Storia dell' iconografia anatomica,* Milan 1957; C.E. Kellett, *Mannerism and medical illustration,* Newcastle 1966; Edwin Clarke and Kenneth Dewhurst, *An illustrated history of brain function,* Oxford 1972

BOOK ILLUSTRATION

John L. Thornton and C. Reeves, *Medical book illustration,* Cambridge 1983; Robert Herrlinger, *History of medical illustration from antiquity to A.D. 1600,* London 1970 (translated from German edition, Munich 1967), continued by Marielene Putscher, *Geschichte der medizinischen Abbildung, von 1660 bis zur Gegenwart,* Munich 1972; Dietrich Brandenburg, *Islamic miniature painting in medical manuscripts,* Basel 1982

CARICATURES

Eugen Holländer, *Die Karikatur und Satire in der Medizin,* second edition, Stuttgart 1921; Cornelis Veth, *De arts in de caricatuur,* Amsterdam n.d.; British Museum, *Catalogue of [British] political and personal satires 1320-1832,* by F.G. Stephens and M.D. George, London 1870-1954 (reprinted 1978); Henri Mondor, *Les gens de médecine dans l'oeuvre de Daumier,* Paris 1960; William H. Helfand and Sergio Rocchietta, *Medicina e farmacia nelle caricature politiche italiane 1848-1914,* Rome 1982

CHEMOTHERAPY

David L. Cowen and A.B. Segelman, *Antibiotics in historical perspective,* [Rahway, New Jersey] 1981

CLINICAL MEDICINE

Helmut Vogt, *Der Arzt am Krankenbett,* Munich 1984

DENTISTRY

Curt Proskauer, *Iconographia odontologica,* Berlin 1926, second, enlarged edition, Hildesheim 1967; H.E. Lässig and R.A. Müller, *Die Zahnheilkunde in Kunst- und Kulturgeschichte,* Cologne 1983; Malvin E. Ring, *Dentistry, an illustrated history,* New York 1985

DISEASES (symptoms in the living patient, in general)

Helmut Vogt, *Das Bild des Kranken. Die Darstellung äusserer Veränderungen durch innere Leiden und ihrer Heilmassnahmen von der Renaissance bis in unsere Zeit,* Munich 1969 (second impression Munich 1980); Susanne Dahm, *Frühe Krankenbildnisse,* Cologne 1981

DISEASES (in particular)

goitre Franz Merke, *History and iconography of endemic goitre and cretinism,* Bern 1984 (translation of German language-edition, Bern 1971) **leprosy** Peter Richards, *The mediaeval leper and his northern heirs,* Cambridge 1977 **mental disease** Sander L. Gilman, *Seeing the insane,* New York 1982; S.L. Gilman, *The face of madness,* New York 1976 **plague (including the "Black Death")** Raymond Crawfurd, *Plague and pestilence in literature and art,* Oxford 1914; *Venezia e la peste 1348-1797,* Venice 1979; *Kos,* 1985, **2,** no. 18, special issue on plague **rabies** Jean Théodorides, *Histoire de la rage: cave canem,* Paris 1986, Lise Wilkinson, 'Understanding the nature of rabies: an historical perspective', in J.B. Campbell and K.M. Charlton (eds.), *Rabies,* Boston 1988, pp. 1-23 **syphilis** Karl Sudhoff, *Graphische und typographische Erstlinge der Syphilisliteratur,* Munich 1912; W.B. Ober, 'To cast a pox. The iconography of syphilis', *American Journal of Dermatology,* 1989, **11:** 74-86

DRUG ADDICTION

Gisela Völger and Karin von Welck (editors), *Rausch und Realität, Drogen im Kulturvergleich,* second edition, Hamburg 1982

HOSPITALS

Casimir Tollet, *Les édifices hospitaliers depuis leur origine jusqu'à nos jours,* second edition, Paris 1892; John D. Thompson and Grace Goldin, *The hospital,* New Haven 1975

INSTRUMENTS

Elisabeth Bennion, *Antique medical instruments,* London 1979; Audrey Davis and Toby Appel, *Bloodletting instruments in the National Museum of History and Technology,* Washington D.C. 1979

MEDIAEVAL MEDICINE AND SURGERY

Loren C. MacKinney, *Medical illustrations in medieval manuscripts,* London 1965; Marie-José Imbault-Huart and others, *La médecine au moyen age à travers les manuscrits de la Bibliothèque Nationale,* Paris 1983; Peter Murray Jones, *Medieval medical miniatures,* London 1984

MEDICINE IN WORKS OF FINE-ART

Jean-Martin Charcot and Paul Richer, *Les difformes et les malades dans l'art,* Paris 1889; Eugen Holländer, *Die Medizin in der klassischen Malerei,* third edition, Stuttgart 1923; Hans Schadewaldt and others, *Kunst und Medizin,* Cologne 1967; J.B. Bedaux, 'Minnekoorts-, zwangerschaps- en doodsverschijnselen op zeventiende-eeuwse schilderijen', *Antiek,* 1975, **10:** 17-42; William Schupbach, *The paradox of Rembrandt's 'Anatomy of Dr Tulp',* London 1982; Diane R. Karp, *Ars medica. Art, medicine and the human condition,* Philadelphia 1985

ICONOGRAPHIC COLLECTIONS

NURSING

John W. Forsaith, *'The lady with the lamp'*, s.l. 1973 (typescript circulated in five copies); M. Patricia Donahue, *Nursing, the finest art*, St Louis 1985; M. Masson, *A pictorial history of nursing*, Twickenham 1985

OBSTETRICS

Gustave J.A. Witkowski, *Histoire des accouchements chez tous les peuples*, Paris 1887, and *Les accouchements dans les beaux-arts*, Paris 1894; Friedrich von Zglinicki, *Geburt*, Braunschweig 1983

PATHOLOGY

Edgar Goldschmid, *Entwicklung und Bibliographie der pathologisch-anatomischen Abbildung*, Leipzig 1925

PHARMACY

Rudolf Schmitz, *Mörser, Kolben und Phiolen. Aus der Welt der Pharmazie*, Stuttgart 1966; Marie-Odile Andrade, *Pharmacies de toujours*, Le Puy 1979; H.A. Bosman-Jelgersma, *Poeders, pillen en patienten*, Amsterdam 1983

PHOTOGRAPHS

Stanley B. Burns, *Early medical photography in America (1839-83)*, New York 1983; Rima D. Apple, *Illustrated catalogue of the slide archive of historical medical photographs at Stony Brook*, Westport, Conn., 1984; Daniel M. Fox and C. Lawrence, *Photographing medicine*, Westport, Conn., 1988

PORTRAITURE

Johann Carl Wilhelm Moehsen, *Verzeichnis einer Samlung von Bildnissen, gröstentheils berühmter Aerzte*, Berlin 1771; W. Drugulin, *Verzeichniss von sechstausend Portraits von Aerzten, Naturforschern, Mathematikern*, Leipzig 1863; William Coolidge Lane and N.E. Browne, *A.L.A. portrait index*, Washington D.C. 1906; Porträtarchiv Diepenbroick, Westfälisches Landesmuseum für Kunst und Kulturgeschichte, Münster, *Der Arzt*, Münster 1979; T.J. Pettigrew, *Medical portrait gallery*, London 1838-1840; Albin Hildebrand and Alfred Levertin, *Svenska Läkaresällskapets 1808-1908*, Stockholm 1909 (not limited to Swedish subjects); Bruno Kisch, 'Iconographies of medical portraits', *Journal of the History of medicine*, 1957, **12**: 366-387; Julius Pagel, *Biographisches Lexikon hervorragender Ärzte des neunzehnten Jahrhunderts*, Berlin 1901, continued by August Hirsch and others, *Biographisches Lexikon der hervorragenden Ärzte aller Zeiten und Völker*, second edition by F. Hübotter, H. Vierordt and W. Haberling, Berlin 1929-1935, and by I. Fischer, *Biographisches Lexikon der hervorragenden Ärzte der letzten fünfzig Jahre*, Berlin 1932-1933 **n.b.** there is no known portrait of Robert Hooke F.R.S. (1635-1703) or of James Parkinson M.D. (1755-1824)

QUACKS

Grete de Francesco, *Die Macht des Charlatans*, Basel 1937

SPECTACLES, EYE-GLASSES etc.

Mme Alfred Heymann, *Lunettes et lorgnettes de jadis,* Paris 1911; W. Poulet, *The arts and spectacles over five centuries,* Bonn 1980

SURGERY

Guido Majno, *The healing hand,* Cambridge, Mass., 1975; Pierre Huard and M.D. Grmek, *Le premier manuscrit chirurgical turc rédigé par Charaf Ed-Din (1465),* Paris 1960; Gert Carstensen and others, *Die Chirurgie in der Kunst,* Düsseldorf 1983 **gynaecological surgery** James V. Ricci, *The development of gynaecological surgery and instruments,* Philadelphia 1949

Relevant current JOURNALS include *Medical History* (London), which publishes 'Illustrations from the Wellcome Institute Library'; *Journal of the History of Medicine* (currently Farmington, Connecticut); *Isis* (Philadelphia); *Medizinhistorisches Journal* (Mainz and Stuttgart); and *Kos* (Florence and Milan). Illustrated non-current journals include *Nouvelle iconographie de la Salpêtrière* (Paris 1888-1918) and *Aesculape* (1911-1968). Many of the forty-two volumes (to date) in the monograph series *Kölner medizinhistorische Beiträge* (Cologne 1977-) are devoted to medico-historical iconography: they are listed in *Zusammenhang. Festschrift für Marielene Putscher,* edited by Otto Baur and Otto Glandien, Cologne 1984, vol. 2, pp. 986-990.

(c) a brief list of selected primary books of medical iconography
(Examples only: for a more comprehensive guide to clinical subjects see Helmut Vogt, *Das Bild des Kranken,* Munich 1969 (second impression Munich 1980).)

GENERAL

Robert James, *A medicinal dictionary,* London 1743-1745; Denis Diderot and J. Le R. d'Alembert, *Encyclopédie, ou dictionnaire raisonné des sciences, des arts et des métiers,* "Paris" 1762-1772

ANATOMY

Andreas Vesalius, *De humani corporis fabrica,* Basel 1543 (but for most purposes the edition of the woodcuts by J.B. de C.M. Saunders and Charles D. O'Malley, *The illustrations from the works of Andreas Vesalius of Brussels,* Cleveland and New York 1950, or the facsimile edition of the *De humani corporis fabrica,* Brussels 1970, should be consulted instead); Jean-Marc Bourgéry and N.H. Jacob, *Traité complet de l'anatomie de l'homme comprenant la médecine opératoire,* Paris 1831-1854; David Waterston, *The Edinburgh stereoscopic atlas of anatomy,* Edinburgh 1905

DENTISTRY

Claudius Ash and Sons Ltd., *Catalogue of artificial teeth* [*etc.*], London 1886-1887

DISEASES (in the living patient, in general)

Karl Heinrich Baumgärtner. *Physiognomice pathologica. Kranken-physiognomik,* Stuttgart and Leipzig 1839 (second edition Stuttgart 1842, third edition Radeburg 1929); Byrom Bramwell, *Atlas of clinical medicine,* Edinburgh 1891-1896

DISEASES (in particular)

cholera Robert Froriep, *Symptome der asiatischen Cholera,* Weimar 1832; Thomas Shapter, *The history of the cholera in Exeter in 1832,* London 1849 **leprosy** Daniel Cornelius Danielssen and Carl Wilhelm Boeck, *Om spedalskhed . . . Atlas,* Bergen 1847 **mental disease** H. Dagonet, *Nouveau traité élémentaire et pratique des maladies mentales,* Paris 1876; *Nouvelle iconographie de la Salpêtrière,* Paris 1888-1918; Wilhelm Weygandt, *Atlas und Grundriss der Psychiatrie,* Munich 1902 **rheumatic disease** Robert Adams, *A treatise on rheumatic gout, or chronic rheumatic arthritis of all the joints* accompanied by *Illustrations of the effects of rheumatic gout, or chronic rheumatic arthritis, on all the articulations* (mainly from *post-mortem* drawings) London 1857, second edition London 1873; Alfred Baring Garrod, *The nature and treatment of gout and rheumatic gout,* London 1859 and later editions **scurvy** Karl Albert Ludwig Aschoff and W.K. Koch, *Skorbut,* Jena 1919 **skin diseases (including dermatological symptoms of venereal diseases)** Jean-Louis Alibert, *Description des maladies de la peau,* Paris 1806; Thomas Bateman, *Delineations of cutaneous diseases,* London 1817; Alexander John Balmanno Squire, *Photographs (coloured from life) of the diseases of the skin,* London 1864-1866 **smallpox** Thomas Frank Ricketts, *The diagnosis of smallpox,* London 1908 **yellow fever** Etienne Pariset, *Observations sur la fièvre jaune,* Paris 1820

HOSPITALS

Henry C. Burdett, *Hospitals and asylums of the world,* London 1891-1893; Dankwart Leistikow, *Ten centuries of European hospital architecture,* Ingelheim am Rhein 1967; Horace Swete, *Handy book of cottage hospitals,* London 1870 **mental hospitals, lunatic asylums etc.** William P. Letchworth, *The insane in foreign countries,* New York 1889

INSTRUMENTS

Joannes Scultetus, *Cheiroplotheke, seu armamentarium chirurgicum,* Ulm 1655, enlarged edition Leiden 1693; Johann Alexander Brambilla, *Instrumentarium chirurgicum viennense,* Vienna 1780; G. Gaujot and E. Spillmann, *Arsenal de la chirurgie contemporaire,* Paris 1867-1872; trade-catalogues of manufacturers e.g. Allen and Hanbury, Arnold and Sons, Down Bros., Savigny, J. Weiss

MATERIA MEDICA

Leonhard Fuchs, *De historia stirpium commentarii insignes,* Basel 1542; Robert Bentley and H. Trimen, *Medicinal plants,* London 1880

MICROBIOLOGY

Antonie van Leeuwenhoek, *Arcana naturae,* Leiden 1708 and other editions

OBSTETRICS

William Hunter, *Anatomia uteri humani gravidi,* Birmingham 1774; Jacques Pierre Maygrier, *Nouvelles démonstrations d'accouchemens,* Paris 1822; François Joseph Moreau, *Traité pratique des accouchemens,* Paris 1837 [1839]

OPHTHALMOLOGY

Georg Bartisch, *Ophthalmodouleia,* Dresden 1583; O. Haab, *Atlas der äusseren Erkrankungen des Auges,* Munich 1899

ORTHOPAEDICS

Nicolas Andry de Boisregard, *L'orthopédie,* Paris 1741; J.M. Delpech, *De l'orthomorphie,* Paris 1828-1829; Lewis A. Sayre, *Spinal disease and spinal curvature,* London 1877

PATHOLOGY

Jean Cruveilhier, *Anatomie pathologique du corps humain,* Paris 1824-1842; Alfred Kast, *Pathologisch-anatomische Tafeln,* Leipzig 1910

PORTRAITURE

Jean-Jacques Boissard, *Icones et effigies,* Frankfurt 1645-1650; John Leyland, *Contemporary medical men and their professional work,* Leicester 1888; Burkhard Reber, *Gallerie hervorragender Therapeutiker und Pharmakognosten der Gegenwart,* Geneva 1897; Anton Mansch, *Medical world. Gallery of contemporaries in the field of medical science,* Berlin c. 1913 (several different editions)

RADIOLOGY

David Walsh, *The Röntgen rays in medical work,* London 1897; Francis H. Williams, *The Roentgen rays in medicine and surgery,* New York 1903

SURGERY (AND DISEASES TREATED BY IT)

Ambroise Paré, *Les oeuvres,* Paris 1575; Gulielmus Fabricius Hildanus, *Opera quae extant omnia,* Frankfurt 1646; Lorenz Heister, *Institutiones chirurgicae,* Amsterdam 1739; Charles Bell, *Illustrations of the great operations of surgery,* London 1821; Ludwig Friedrich Froriep and Robert Froriep, *Chirurgische Kupfertafeln,* Weimar 1820-1847; Bourgéry and Jacob, *op. cit.* (see ANATOMY, p. 65 above); Claude Bernard and Charles Huette, *Précis iconographique de médecine opératoire,* Paris 1853; William Watson Cheyne, *Antiseptic surgery,* London 1882 **ovariotomy** A. Krassowsky, *Ob ovariotomii,* St Petersburg 1868 **amputation** Joseph Sampson Gamgee, *History of a successful case of amputation at the hip-joint . . . with four photographs by Sarony and Pierre-Petit,* London 1865.

SOME FACILITIES AND SERVICES

The preservation and use of the Iconographic Collections would be impossible without the aid of expert staff serving the different departments of the Library. Their work enables the Wellcome Institute to provide a wide range of services, both in Britain and abroad.

CONSERVATION

Among the skills of the paper conservators, those which apply particularly to the Iconographic Collections include the ability to release drawings and prints from the acidic boards on which they were often laid down in the past. Some of these boards are shown in the foreground of the photograph, while the print held up on the right has been re-mounted on acid-free board with a window-mount which should protect it from some forms of physical damage in the future.

ICONOGRAPHIC COLLECTIONS

The paintings conservators take care of such matters as the atmospheric control of paintings, cleaning away yellowed varnish, removing discoloured retouchings, and making good any losses of paint. In the photograph, small abrasions on a sixteenth-century panel painting are retouched with a very fine brush. In the background, newly cleaned, is the painting reproduced on the front cover of this booklet.

PHOTOGRAPHY

Thanks to the work of the Library's Photographic Service, the Iconographic Collections are available to scholars, students, lecturers, publishers and the public in the form of photographic prints and slides.

EXHIBITIONS

The Iconographic Collections contribute to exhibitions both at the Wellcome Institute and in other venues. Thematic exhibitions at the Institute clarify the Library's holdings on given subjects, and their catalogues are works of reference of permanent value. Above, an exhibition on historical aspects of anaesthesia, held at the Wellcome Institute in connection with the Second International Symposium on the History of Anaesthesia, London 1987.

In the six months before the publication of this booklet, pictures were lent from the Iconographic Collections to exhibitions in Cambridge, Colchester, Dublin, Finland and the United States. Above, a poster exhibition organized by the Iconographic Collections staff was displayed at the workshop on "The Natural History of Schizophrenia" (Schizophrenia Research Foundation) in Madras, February 1989, and inaugurated by Professor M.G.K. Menon FRS, Scientific Advisor to the Prime Minister of India. (Photograph reproduced by kind permission of Dr S. Rajkumar).

PUBLICATIONS

    The pictures in the Iconographic Collections are reproduced frequently in publications both scholarly and popular: monographs, journals, films, magazines etc. While the Library itself is open to visitors only in ordinary office-hours, the international audience for these publications forms an additional, largely hidden, constituency which uses the Library's resources round the clock.

Printed on 25 September 1989
by Libra Printing of Datchet, Berkshire,
on their presses at Thetford, Norfolk, England